ENDING CHILD POVERTY

Popular welfare for the 21st century?

Edited by Robert Walker

First published in Great Britain in 1999 by

The Policy Press
University of Bristol
34 Tyndall's Park Road
Bristol BS8 1PY
UK

Tel   +44 (0)117 954 6800
Fax   +44 (0)117 973 7308
E-mail tpp@bristol.ac.uk
http://www.bristol.ac.uk/Publications/TPP

ISBN 1 86134 199 7

Robert Walker is Director of the Centre for Research in Social Policy and the Social Security Unit, Loughborough University and Professor of Social Policy Research.

Cover design by Qube Design Associates, Bristol.
Photograph on front cover kindly supplied by Keith Saunders/Arena Images.
Printed in Great Britain by Hobbs the Printers Ltd, Southampton.

Contents

Notes on contributors

Tony Atkinson is Warden of Nuffield College and was formerly Professor of Economics at the University of Cambridge, London School of Economics, University College London and Essex. He is a member of the Conseil d'Analyse Economique.

Tony Blair was elected Leader of the Labour Party in 1994 and became Prime Minister of the United Kingdom on 2 May 1997. He is the Member of Parliament for Sedgefield.

Robin Butler is Master of University College, Oxford, and was formerly Secretary of the Cabinet and Head of the Home Civil Service. He sits on the Cross Benches in the House of Lords.

Simon Cross is Tutor in Communication and Media Studies and Research Officer in the Communication Research Centre at Loughborough University.

Alan Deacon is Professor of Social Policy and a member of the ESRC Research Group for the study of Care, Values and the Future of Welfare at the University of Leeds.

Anthony Giddens is Director of the London School of Economics and Political Science and was previously Professor of Sociology at the University of Cambridge.

Peter Golding is Head of the Department of Social Sciences and Professor of Sociology at Loughborough University. He is a member of the Executive Committee of the Child Poverty Action Group.

Jose Harris is Professor of Modern History and Leverhulme Research Professor at the University of Oxford. She is author of the standard account of Beveridge's life and thought.

John Hills is the Director of the ESRC Research Centre for Analysis of Social Exclusion and Professor of Social Policy at the London School of Economics. He was formerly Co-Director of the London School of Economics' Welfare State Programme.

Bob Holman was formerly Professor of Social Policy at the University of Bath. For the last 22 years he has lived in and worked with local neighbourhood projects in two deprived areas.

Peter Kellner is a political columnist for the *London Evening Standard*, and contributor to the *Observer, New Statesman,* Newsnight (BBC TV) and Analysis (BBC Radio Four).

Julian Le Grand is the Richard Titmuss Professor of Social Policy at the London School of Economics.

Ruth Lister is Professor of Social Policy at Loughborough University. She is a former director of the Child Poverty Action Group and member of the Commission on Social Justice.

David Piachaud is Professor of Social Policy at the London School of Economics. He has worked at the Department of Health and Social Security (1968-70) and the Prime Minister's Policy Unit (1974-79).

Raymond Plant is Master of St Catherine's College Oxford until 31 December 1999. From January 2000 he will become Professor of European Political Thought at the University of Southampton. He sits as a Labour member of the House of Lords.

Polly Toynbee is a columnist on *The Guardian*, formerly columnist and Associate Editor of *The Independent*, and BBC Social Affairs Editor 1989-96.

Robert Walker is Director of the Centre for Research in Social Policy and the Social Security Unit, Loughborough University and Professor of Social Policy Research.

Acknowledgements

Sincere thanks are due to Sharon White and David Miliband of the Prime Minister's Policy Unit for their encouragement and support; to the contributors for agreeing to the publication of notes and papers that were never intended for public consumption; and to Sharon Walker, Suella Harriman, Lynne Cox and Jenny Park for producing and proofreading the manuscript.

Thanks are also due to Wilf Stevenson and the Smith Institute for permission to reprint Polly Toynbee's chapter from W. Stevenson, *Equality and the modern economy; Seminar 2: Making welfare work*, originally published in London by the Smith Institute in 1998.

Foreword

In my experience, this book is a unique event. I am delighted to have been invited to write a foreword to it.

I invited the Prime Minister, the Rt Hon Tony Blair MP, to give a lecture on 'Beveridge re-visited: a welfare state for the 21st century' to launch a lecture series commemorating the 750th anniversary of the endowment of University College, Oxford – the oldest recorded foundation of higher education in the English-speaking world.

The grounds for the invitation were that William Beveridge wrote his report of 1942 while he was Master of University College. He was assisted in its preparation by Harold Wilson, then a Fellow of University College and afterwards Labour Prime Minister, and the report was implemented under the 1945-51 government led by Clement Attlee, also an Old Member of University College.

It was appropriate that Attlee's and Wilson's successor as Prime Minister and leader of a government pledged to the reform of the welfare state should review Beveridge's achievement and describe the approach of his own government.

This was bound to be an important occasion, and the Prime Minister and his advisers took it seriously. Tony Blair had not spoken extensively on the subject as Prime Minister and it provided an opportunity to set out his thinking at an early stage of his government.

The importance of this book is that it includes a range of contributions by distinguished experts in the field which were available to the Prime Minister when his lecture was being prepared. It is therefore possible not only to read the ideas of leading current thinkers in this crucial area of policy but also to compare them with the Prime Minister's lecture, and see which ideas he himself took up and in what form.

This is what makes the book unique. In due course it will be possible to see also the fate of the approach in the Prime Minister's lecture – the extent to which it was implemented and the extent to which it was effective. Meanwhile, this book is a record not only of the lecture itself but also of the ideas available to the government and their influence on its leader at an important moment in the formation of policy. I am delighted that the occasion of this lecture triggered a very productive channel of communication between academics and policy makers – something which I have worked for many years to promote.

Lord Butler of Brockwell GCG CVO
Master of University College, Oxford

Section 1
Welfare for the 21st century

ONE

Introduction

Robert Walker

On 18 March 1999, the occasion of the 750th anniversary of University College, Oxford, Tony Blair, the British Prime Minister, delivered the Beveridge Lecture in which he set out his own vision of a welfare state for the 21st century. In this lecture, reproduced here as Chapter 2, Tony Blair reflects on Beveridge the man, his times and the reforms that he initiated that were to lay the foundation for welfare in the second half of the 20th century. He goes on to consider the profound social changes that have reshaped modern society over the last 50 years and the apparent failure of the welfare policies to respond sufficiently to prevent the growth of poverty, social decay and social exclusion. The present-day welfare state, he concludes, is not fitted for the modern world. Indeed, it is seen by some to be the social problem rather than a solution to social needs. Finally, and most importantly, he articulates a new vision for the future that is perhaps as challenging as the blueprint laid down by Beveridge.

Despite the importance of Blair's Beveridge Lecture, it is not surprising that it did not attract the attention accorded to the Beveridge Report with its detailed programme of reform that caught the popular imagination in wartime Britain and provided a glimpse of a better world to come. Competing with the war in Kosovo and the murder of a Northern Ireland civil rights lawyer, coverage of the Beveridge Lecture was very largely limited to the print medium. Moreover, in today's world, neither poverty, nor policy on poverty, is news unless there is at least the hint of political discord (see Simon Cross and Peter Golding in Chapter 16). In fact, Blair's new commitment in the Lecture to end child poverty within 20 years was met with a considerable degree of accord in both the tabloids and the broadsheets. There was discussion about the appropriateness of the time-scale and about the absence of a precise definition of poverty and, in some quarters, a world-weary scepticism about Labour's true intentions, but little direct hostility. Equally, though, there was little discussion of the strategy for eradicating child poverty, something that Blair often dealt with only at the level of principle.

Whether history accords Blair's Beveridge Lecture the same importance as the original Beveridge Report will depend on the public's response to it. Whereas Beveridge offered a blueprint for reform based on popular support, if not consensus, Tony Blair provides a vision supported by the reforms that Labour has introduced since coming to power. For Blair to be able to translate his vision into a blueprint, or even a sketch map for future development of welfare, requires both popular support for radical reform and further detailed policy proposals.

A necessary precondition for both is an informed public debate about Blair's analysis of current social problems and his aspirations for the future. Is he right that welfare in its current form is not working, that this is because society has changed faster than policy, that radical reform is necessary and that there is adequate agreement about the objectives of reform and of the welfare state in the 21st century?

In publishing Blair's Beveridge Lecture alongside the views of some of Britain's leading policy analysts and commentators on welfare reform, the aim is to stimulate critical debate about the future shape of British welfare.

The contributions presented Section 2 of the volume provide a themed context for the Beveridge Lecture. They were written in January and February 1999, before Blair presented his lecture, and have been modified, where appropriate, to take account of policy changes announced in the 1999 Budget.

Within the overall remit of considering Beveridge's legacy and ideas, and how the welfare state should be reformed to meet modern needs, contributors were asked to do slightly different things. Jose Harris, Tony Atkinson and John Hills were asked to write about Beveridge, the man and his ideas, and the applicability of Beveridge's approach to welfare in the 21st century. Peter Kellner was requested, in addition, to think about the need to update Beveridge in the context of the 'third way' and the need for fresh thinking about Labour and equality. A number including Julian Le Grand, Anthony Giddens and Raymond Plant were to focus especially on modern conceptions of social justice and their application to modern welfare. Alan Deacon was specifically asked to consider how rights and responsibilities should be balanced in combating poverty and social justice and Piachaud was asked for a critique of New Right thinking. Yet others had to reflect on the successes and failures of policy over the past half century (Robert Walker), or during the period since Labour had come to power in May 1997 (Ruth Lister).

The contributors also vary in their interpretation of their respective tasks but all retain an emphasis on succinctness. Some have kept closely to their brief; others have been tempted to sketch out a blueprint of their own. David Piachaud has added a critique of the New Left to complement that on the New Right. Raymond Plant initially produced two notes that have been merged for publication. Polly Toynbee also made two submissions, the second of which offered an elaboration on the first which is published here, the transcript of a talk given at a Smith Institute seminar (which took place on 20 May 1998 at 11 Downing Street). Others have restricted their contributions to pertinent personal reflections, often telling in their power to persuade. The result is a rich tapestry of analysis, insight and reflection that provides an initial datum against which to assess Blair's vision of welfare.

The final section of the volume is a direct response to the Beveridge Lecture. Simon Cross and Peter Golding, in Chapter 16, review the media coverage that the Lecture received, identify the main issues and angles that emerged, and assess the tone of the initial reaction.

Chapter 17 compares the content of the lecture with that of the other contributors to the volume. It identifies shared themes and areas of disagreement. It relates Blair's analysis of the motors for reform to those suggested by welfare specialists, looks for common ground on the objectives of reform and begins to expand and refine the strategies and options for reform.

Like the volume as a whole, the final chapter engages the academic and policy community with the ideas and ideals of the leader of a reforming government. While one would not expect to find universal accord, such dialogue can be a recipe for constructive government and a stimulus to open debate about issues that are important to every citizen and to democracy itself.

TWO

Beveridge revisited: a welfare state for the 21st century[1]

Tony Blair

Today I want to talk to you about a great challenge: how we make the welfare state popular again. How we restore public trust and confidence in a welfare state that 50 years ago was acclaimed but today has so many wanting to bury it. I will argue that the only road to 'a popular welfare state' is radical welfare reform.

And I will set out our historic aim that ours is the first generation to end child poverty forever, and it will take a generation. It is a 20-year mission but I believe it can be done.

It is worth recapping briefly on the enormous amount of reform now underway. Partly because the Opposition aren't quite sure what to say about it, it has been less controversial than many anticipated. But those who predicted timidity have been proven wholly wrong. In two years we have:

- reformed the whole of student finance;
- introduced the largest programme for the young unemployed ever put in place in Britain;
- published, and are now legislating, the Welfare Reform Bill that will modernise the whole of disability provision, benefit claims and support in bereavement and introduce stakeholder pensions;
- set out a framework for future pension reform that will alter the entirety of pension provision over the next 20 years, while introducing the Minimum Income Guarantee for today's pensioners;
- made radical proposals to reform the Child Support Agency and the whole of legal aid;
- and of course, we are changing, through the Working Families Tax Credit, the new Family Credit and 20% increase in Child Benefit, the whole of provision for children and for families.

And we are now turning our attention to long-term care and Housing Benefit. It is the fullest programme of reform of any government this century.

And I believe it is wholly in the spirit of Beveridge.

Beveridge the man

Beveridge was perhaps the greatest British social reformer of the 20th century. He was a brilliant but difficult man. He devoted his life to understanding and abolishing poverty, starting here at Toynbee Hall. He was a remarkable talent and enthusiast. Permanent Secretary at 39. And able to say at 80 that "I am still radical and young enough to believe that mountains can be moved". He was in the Liberal Party but really a forerunner of modern social democracy, arguing for top-class public services for all. When people ask me why I favour stronger links between Labour and the Liberal Democrats, I say and mean that my lexicon of political heroes include Keynes and Beveridge, alongside Keir Hardie, Bevan and Attlee.

Beveridge laid the foundations of the modern welfare state. His plan, published in 1942, heralded the first British comprehensive system of free healthcare; universal family support; and rights to minimum rates of social insurance benefits during old age or in the event of unemployment, sickness or disability. It transformed Britain for the better. It improved the health of the nation and in large measure removed absolute poverty and destitution from our country. It was an enormous step change, ending the lottery of state welfare that had existed since the Poor Law.

But, as Tony Atkinson has said, Beveridge would have been 'profoundly irritated' by any assumption that his plan could serve the needs of the 21st century as well as it has served the 20th century. His views were constantly evolving, constantly changing to meet new needs.

Social change

Social justice is as relevant today as it was for Beveridge. It is our aim. It is our central belief – the basis for a community where everyone has the chance to succeed.

Social justice is about decency. It requires that any citizen of our society should be able to meet their needs for income, housing, health and education.

Social justice is about merit. It demands that life chances should depend on talent and effort, not the chance of birth; and that talent and effort should be handsomely rewarded. The child born on a run-down housing estate should have the same chance to be healthy and well-educated as the child born in the leafy suburbs. It is only when you put it like that that you see the distance we have to go.

Social justice is about mutual responsibility. It insists that we all accept duties as well as rights – to each other and to society.

Social justice is about fairness. In a community founded on social justice, power, wealth and opportunity will be the hands of the many not the few. These words come from the new Clause IV of the Labour Party constitution and they are what New Labour is about.

Social justice is about values. The values are timeless. But their application must change with changing times. That is why it is *New Labour*.

As John Hills has written, Beveridge's plan for the 'abolition of want' was based on his reading of research on the nature of poverty and society in the 1930s. His solution was tailored to fit the needs of the day. In the last 60 years the world has changed dramatically. It would be surprising, lazy even, to believe that the solutions that suited a post-war Britain could work just as well in today's global economy.

Most strikingly, the position of women has changed. Beveridge drew on the 1931 Census to argue that:

> **More than seven out of eight of all housewives, that is to say married women of working age, made marriage their sole occupation, less than one in eight of all housewives was also gainfully occupied.**

He assumed that after the war, when women had worked in far greater numbers, the world would remain the same. But it didn't. Sixty years on, women's lives have been transformed. Half the workforce is made up of women. And Beveridge would have been amazed that one in five of all families with children was headed by a lone parent.

Our society has aged. This would have surprised Beveridge less. Only 10% of the population was over state pension age in 1931. In 1991 it was 18%. In 2021 it will be 21%. And while there is no 'demographic timebomb' in Britain, as some would have us believe, we have gradually become an older population.

Work patterns have changed. Beveridge like most of his contemporaries, was committed to full employment, delivered by Keynesian demand management.

The assumption of enduring full employment held good during the 1940s and 1950s when jobs were plentiful, thanks to post-war reconstruction. It didn't matter so much how poorly skilled people were. Work was easy to come by, though in the main, of course, it was men who worked. That assumption began to come apart as early as the 1970s when traditional demand management failed to curb rising unemployment.

Today the assumption has completely broken down. Globalisation has placed a premium on workers with the skills and knowledge to adapt to advancing technology. People without skills find it very hard to compete. If they can find work it is too often short-term and so poorly paid that it does not provide a springboard out of poverty. New groups of unemployed have appeared: people taking early retirement because of incapacity and parents bringing up young children on their own.

By the 1970s it was plain that the welfare state of the first half of the 20th century wasn't going to be right for the second half of the 20th century. One of the key insights of Beveridge was his fundamental belief that the concept of social welfare had to fit economic policy. He fashioned the welfare state around a view of the economy – the full employment, mass production economy of the 1940s.

By the 1970s, economic policy and social policy were becoming divorced. Welfare policy – redistribution, social security – were seen almost as antithetical to sound economic policy. The welfare state was, in certain quarters, being seen as a burden to be paid for at the expense of wealth creation.

The Left, trapped in a false confusion of means and ends, resisted changing the welfare state on the grounds that to modernise the welfare state was to undermine it. Social justice became, on the Left, identified with rigid policy prescriptions, good for the 1940s, increasingly out of date for the 1970s. The Right moved in.

The record of the previous government – failure of the Right

I asked David Piachaud to write a paper in preparation for this speech.
As he points out,

> **... after 18 years of Conservative government there was more poverty – one third of children living in families under half average income levels.**

> **... more inequality between rich and poor.**

... more dependent on benefits, particularly means tested benefits.

... more homeless on the streets.

The Right came to power, committed to cutting welfare costs. The fundamental irony is that it ended up in increasing them. No budget of any department rose more under the last government than social security. This was despite many measures – like ending the link between earnings and pensions – which cut costs.

The reason is simple. Whereas the Old Left regarded the application of social justice as unchanged, the Right regarded it as irrelevant. They believed that it didn't matter, and that it had no connection with economic efficiency. Indeed, it is that curious alliance of the Right and Old Left that I have witnessed and struggled against all my political life; both far Left and Right divorced economic efficiency from social justice. Both saw wealth creation as in opposition to social justice.

The Right were not mistaken about the importance of markets and greater competition. But they failed to see in the modern world that it is not enough.

Keynes wrote of this flawed approach:

> **The Economists were teaching that wealth, commerce and machinery were the children of free competition.... But the Darwinians could go one better than that – free competition had built Man. The human eye was no longer the demonstration of (God's) design, miraculously contriving all things for the best; it was the supreme achievement of Chance, operating under conditions of free competition and laissez-faire. The principle of the Survival of the Fittest could be regarded as a vast generalisation of Ricardian economics. Socialistic interferences became, in the light of this grander synthesis, not merely inexpedient, but impious, as calculated to retard the onward movement of the mighty process by which we ourselves had risen like Aphrodite out of the primeval slime of the Ocean.**

So, under the last government, social security spending went up, but poverty and social exclusion went up too. They cut away at the budget, sometimes creating problems along the way, for example, encouraging fraud in their cuts to Housing Benefit. But they failed to tackle the fundamental weaknesses of the welfare state. They left unreformed areas that had become outdated, such as the inadequacy of childcare support for working women. They failed to create a modern welfare state fit for the modern world.

Therefore welfare became unpopular. Welfare, though not the concept of the welfare state, became a term of abuse. It became associated with fraud, abuse, laziness, a dependency culture, social irresponsibility encouraged by welfare dependency. Welfare was blamed as the problem not the solution.

This is dangerous.

For if people lose faith in welfare's ability to deliver, then politicians have an impossible job persuading hard-pressed taxpayers that their money should go on a system that is not working. If all welfare – the good spending as well as the bad – becomes stigmatised, then the security of children, the disabled, pensioners is put at risk.

The welfare state was popular in Beveridge's day. Because Beveridge made it popular. It was associated with progress and achievement. Providing people with their first pension, a decent home, peace of mind when unemployed. Our job is to make the welfare state once again a force for progress. I want to make all of the welfare state as popular as the NHS because it is providing real security and opportunity, because we have rooted out fraud and because we are giving greatest help to those with the greatest needs.

A modern vision of welfare

The third way in welfare is clear: not to dismantle it, or to protect it unchanged, but to reform it radically – taking its core values and applying them to the modern world.

Above all, we must reconnect social justice to economic vision. Our economic vision for Britain in the 21st century is clear: stability in economic management; and then, on that foundation, build the knowledge economy, where we compete by skill, talent and technology. Education is an economic as well as a social imperative. In the Green Paper on Welfare, published last March, we called for a new welfare contract between the citizens of the country based on 'Work for those who can work, security for those who can't'. This means refocusing dramatically the objectives and operation of the welfare state. If the knowledge economy is an aim, then work, skill and above all, investing in children, become essential aims of welfare. Of course, security for those who can't work or who are retired is vital; and big change is needed there too. But a welfare state that is just about 'social security' is inadequate. It is passive where we now need it to be active. It encourages dependency where we need to encourage independence, initiative, enterprise for all.

By linking it to an economic vision, the welfare state, radically reformed, can be popular because everyone, haves and have-nots, can see its raison d'être.

The characteristic of the modern popular welfare state will be the following.

First, it will tackle social exclusion, child poverty, community decay in an active way; and tackle it through tackling the fundamental causes: structural unemployment; poor education; poor housing; the crime and drugs culture. The talent we waste through social exclusion, we waste not just for the individual but for the nation. Let us liberate it and use it for the nation.

Second, welfare will be a hand-up not a hand-out. Mutual responsibility. We have a responsibility to provide young people with life chances. They have a responsibility to take them. Parents have responsibility for their children. Those who can do so have a responsibility to save for their retirement.

The state becomes an enabler, not just a provider. Otherwise the costs are out of control and the consent for the taxpayer to fund welfare declines.

Third, where people really need security, the most help should go to those with the most need.

These will always be a mix of universal and targeted help. But the one is not 'superior' or 'more principled' than the other.

Fourth, we must root out fraud and abuse in any way we can and, as Frank Field has rightly said, not just in individual cases, but by ending the systemic encouragement of fraud in the way the welfare state is designed.

Fifth, the welfare state need no longer be delivered only through the state or through traditional methods of government. Public/private partnership and the voluntary sector will have and should have a greater role to play.

Sixth, welfare is not just about benefits. Active welfare is about services too – schools, hospitals, the whole infrastructure of community support.

What New Labour is doing in government

So that's the vision for a popular welfare state. What are we doing to make it happen? At every level, we are implementing it.

We are getting people back into work. The New Deal embodies the new ethic at the heart of our reforms – mutual responsibilities. It means government offering real opportunities, but people having an obligation to take them or risk losing benefits. 230,000 young people have already joined the programme, and 60,000 are already in jobs. Since we took office long-term unemployment among young people has halved, and the combination of sound economic policies and active policies in the labour market mean that Britain has now created – net – nearly half a million new jobs, a huge advance in opportunities. And we have extended it from the young unemployed to lone parents, the disabled who want to work and to the over 50s. To make the system work better we are introducing a 'single gateway' into the welfare system for all benefit claimants of working age. That means personalised help for people but a requirement that they attend interviews.

Despite some carping from the usual suspects, the New Deal is an extraordinary success. 40,000 employers are signed up. Their biggest complaint is they can't get enough of the New Dealers. The New Dealers' biggest complaint is trying to get on to the New Deal. To the cynics, I say: talk to the young people and the lone parents, thousands of them now in work. The New Deal is no YTS; no skivvy scheme. It is empowerment in action and I am proud of it.

We are making work pay. The Working Families Tax Credit, the minimum wage, the childcare credit, will make work pay for millions of families. Our deal: if you work hard you will not be in poverty. Our guarantee: that if you work full-time you will take home at least £10,000 a year and you will not have to pay any tax until you earn £12,500 a year.

On April 1 this government will introduce Britain's first ever minimum wage. This will be a great landmark for the country. A symbol of fairness. An act of social justice that Beveridge would have been proud to call his own.

We are modernising public services. The £40bn into health and education is money for modernisation. In education we are taking the action needed to turn round our schools so that every parent can rely on a decent education for their children. We are focusing on literacy and numeracy; better pay, recognition and status for teachers; a relentless attack on failure wherever it occurs.

In health we are trying to turn a treasured but often unresponsive health service into a modern, consumer-focused, quality NHS through modern building and equipment, modernised primary care services, proper quality audit and faster care.

We are tackling social decay. £800m in the New Deal for Communities to turn around our poorest housing estates. Action in London and other cities to ensure that no one has to sleep rough on the streets. Measures to stop the truancy and exclusions that mean that thousands leave school without any qualifications. All bringing the different parts of government to work together. All about preventing tomorrow's problems rather than only picking up the pieces from missed opportunities in the past. Bringing hope to communities that had lost hope. We are fostering local and community innovation. Local people know best what they need and how to provide it.

I asked Bob Holman who is a community worker and sociology professor in Glasgow what he thought. He told me of one neighbourhood project in Easterhouse. A woman who started to help out at a local lunch club then became a member of the local cooperative, eventually becoming its chair. As her self-confidence grew she was able again to take custody of her child and is now a respected community activist. It is stories like these that I want to see replicated across the country.

We are providing real security for those who can't work or have retired. Severely disabled people with the greatest needs will get a big increase in income. Pensioners are now benefiting from a guaranteed income that will go up in line with earnings not just prices. Free eye tests are being restored from April. And we are raising the winter allowance to £100 so that today's pensioners can benefit. Real security for those most in need.

And in doing so we are building new public and private partnerships. There needs to be a mixed economy in the funding of welfare comprising the state, private and voluntary sectors. In pensions we are shifting the balance of funding from the state to the private sector. Currently funding is split 60% state, 40% private. This will reverse to 40% state, 60% private, as the less well-off take up the new stakeholder pensions.

But we also need to develop mixed partnerships in the delivery of welfare. We have made a start in the New Deal involving the private providers, the voluntary sector, parents, and we intend to go further.

But above all our welfare reform programme will give children – all children – the support they need. Our approach on children brings together all the lessons we have learned from applying reform in other areas.

We have made children our top priority because, as the Chancellor memorably said in his Budget, "they are 20% of the population but they are 100% of the future".

The levels of child deprivation are frightening:

- almost one in three children in our country lives in poverty;
- poor children are 2½ times more likely to have no qualifications;
- girls from deprived backgrounds are 10 times more likely to have a teenage pregnancy than girls from well-off families;
- poor children are more likely to play truant;
  - more likely to get excluded from school;
  - more likely to get in trouble with the police;
  - more likely to live in a deprived area;
  - more likely to be from an ethnic minority family;
  - more likely to be brought up by one parent.

And in the last 20 years the tax burden on families has increased. At the very time that families have come under increasing pressure, juggling work and home, the state has made it harder than ever for them to cope.

We need to break the cycle of disadvantage so that children born into poverty are not condemned to social exclusion and deprivation. That is why it is so important that we invest in our children.

But our reforms will help more than the poorest children. All parents need help. All children need support.

Across government, children are getting a better deal. Our family policy is geared to children and their well-being more than the type of family that a child is born to. I make no apologies for that. Education is our number one priority because without skills and knowledge children will not succeed in life. And our welfare policy does all that it can to lift children out of poverty at key points in their lives.

Throughout their childhood children are getting the support they need.

At birth families are getting more Child Benefit, a new children's tax credit and extended maternity support.

In the early years, we want all parents to have the chance to spend more time with their children. So we have introduced new rights to parental leave. We want children to be ready to learn when they start school. So we are expanding childcare and nursery care, with a special Sure Start programme for children at particular risk of social exclusion. These new services will also help parents who wish to return to work, supported by the Working Families Tax Credit and minimum wage.

In their school years, we want our children to have the best education possible. That is why we're driving up school standards, tackling failing schools, concentrating on giving children the basic skills of reading, writing and numeracy that they need to get on. But we also want them to have worthwhile activities to go to outside school. There is nothing more dispiriting than seeing a 13-year-old hanging around on the streets with nothing to do. That's why we're bringing in a national network of after-school clubs providing opportunities to learn and play.

Our plans will start by lifting 700,000 children out of poverty by the end of the Parliament. Poverty should not be a birthright. Being poor should not be a life sentence. We need to sow the seeds of ambition in the young.

Our historic aim will be for ours to be the first generation to end child poverty, and it will take a generation. It is a 20-year mission but I believe it can be done.

The results of our reforms

The consequence of these reforms is a quiet revolution. They are being carried through by a quiet revolutionary – Alistair Darling.

We are already beginning to see the results. The messages we send into the system about the importance of work do bear fruit. Since we came to government we have cut the real growth of social security spending by almost 1% a year. In our first two years we have spent over £5bn less than the previous government planned for.

In the future we will increase provision on our priority areas – children, pensioners, disabled people. So we are keeping our promise to cut the bills of social and economic failure, while spending more on education, the NHS and those who really need help.

We will have welfare spending under control.

Good spending on areas we want money spent on – like Child Benefit and pensions – is going up.

Bad spending on the bills of economic failure is coming down.

Spending this Parliament on children will increase by more than £6bn.

We are creating a welfare system which is 'active' not 'passive', genuinely providing people with a 'hand-up' not a 'hand-out'. Previous governments were satisfied simply to dole out money. The Tories spent over £90bn on benefits, but a fraction of that sum on getting people back to work. That is not our approach. We believe that the role of the welfare state is to help people help themselves, to give people the means to be independent. We are creating an active welfare state focused on giving people the opportunities they need to support themselves, principally through work.

'Popular welfare' – part of New Labour's vision for Britain

I believe Beveridge would have been proud of the changes we are making. The aims have not changed. The means are radically reformed. I would go further. I would like to think that he and Keynes would have been proud to be supporters of New Labour, or at least let us say on the cooperative wing of the Liberal Democrats! Both are part of the heritage that today's Labour Party draws upon. That is because Labour has, through New Labour, returned to our roots. At its best, the Centre-Left of politics, and here I include people outside my Party as well as in it, has stood for two things: progress and justice. To be the advocates of the future with fairness. Modernising always, but for a purpose: to build a better, fairer society, where economic prosperity and social justice go hand in hand and where, as the new Clause IV says, we live together freely in a spirit of solidarity, tolerance and respect.

A modern popular welfare state is an integral part of a bigger picture. The vision for Britain under New Labour is:

- a modern economy based on stability and knowledge;
- a modern civic society based on a reformed welfare state;
- a modern constitution which gives more power to the people;
- a modern approach to the world in which Britain loses its post-Empire lack of confidence, and reaches out strong and engaged to play its full part in Europe and the wider world.

It is within our grasp. As the 21st century beckons, it is time to make that vision, and the modern popular welfare state at its heart, a reality.

Note

[1] The Beveridge Lecture was given at Toynbee Hall, London, on 18 March 1999 as part of the celebrations for the 750th Anniversary of University College, Oxford.

Section 2
Contributions

A Beveridge and his legacy

THREE

Beveridge and the Beveridge Report – life, ideas, influence

Jose Harris

The 'myth' of Beveridge

The *Beveridge Report* of 1942 is still seen, not just in Britain, but throughout the world, as the 'Magna Carta' of the welfare state. Modern commentators usually portray it in one of three lights:

1. The Beveridge Plan was grossly extravagant, demoralised the British people with free hand-outs, and swallowed up scarce resources that should have been used for post-war investment and industrial reconstruction. (Beveridge himself is often portrayed by this school of thought as a sinister, sentimental, socialist idealist.)
2. The Plan was excessively spartan and mean, obsessed with the work-ethic, geared to propping-up private property and the free market, and adopted a rock-bottom definition of 'poverty' that reformers have been striving to get rid of ever since. (Beveridge on this view is a cat's-paw of liberal capitalism.)
3. The Plan's support for full employment, a national health service, subsistence-level family allowances, and an equal benefit system for all, laid down clear-cut benchmarks of equality and justice that have long been lost sight of – hence the muddle, inadequacy and demoralisation of the current welfare state, which can only be cured by a strategy of 'back-to-Beveridge'. (Beveridge himself here seen as a great humanitarian social reformer on a par with Florence Nightingale.)

The man and his career

Who and what lay behind these extraordinarily conflicting reputations? William Beveridge had pursued a single-minded personal mission to understand and abolish poverty ever since 1903, when he left Oxford (with a triple-first-class degree in mathematics and classics) to work in the East End settlement, Toynbee Hall. He there wrote his seminal book on *Unemployment* (1909), which ascribed it mainly to the failure of employers and public authorities to 'organise' the labour market and to encourage mobility, information, work incentives and occupational training. His ideas were taken up by the Fabian socialists, Sidney and Beatrice Webb, and in 1908 he was recruited at their recommendation by the new Liberal minister, Winston Churchill, onto the Board of Trade. There Beveridge was largely responsible for preparing the Labour Exchanges and National Insurance Acts that were to be of seminal importance in the evolution of state welfare. The National Insurance Act (1911) was based on a three-way administrative partnership between government, employers, and non-profit-making voluntary organisations: for the first time working men and women became contractually entitled to basic state benefits (other than the Poor Law) during sickness and unemployment and to rudimentary free healthcare – all of which they were encouraged to supplement with additional voluntary provision. Beveridge himself thereafter rose meteorically through the civil service, and was a major figure in Lloyd George's wartime Ministry of Munitions before becoming in 1918, at the age of 39, Permanent Secretary of the Ministry of Food. Nevertheless, his career during the First World War may be seen as illustrating a point made by Harold Wilson, that Beveridge was "undoubtedly the greatest administrative genius of this century, but almost certainly the worst administrator". In other words, he did not suffer fools gladly, constantly fretted against red tape, and lost his temper with people who disagreed with him – be they business men who resisted rationing and profit controls, trade unionists who clung to the union rule book in the deepest depths of wartime crisis, and everyone who opposed greater extension of social insurance and state regulation of the labour market. By 1919 he was widely seen as a sinister 'Germanising' influence in British government, wholly out of tune with the widespread 'dismantling of controls' and reversion to 'normality' that set in at the end of the war. He therefore accepted the post of Director of the London School of Economics, which, over the next 18 years, he transformed from a small and obscure college for part-time students into one of the most important centres for the social sciences in the world. Again, however, his imperious methods offended many of his colleagues, and in 1937 he moved on to the mastership of University College, Oxford – convinced that British society was too obstinate, corrupt and pig-headed to be reformed on rational lines, and looking forward to a tranquil old age of private research and retirement.

Beveridge's political beliefs

Beveridge is usually seen (and saw himself) as a Liberal, but nevertheless he was a Liberal of a rather particular kind. In other words, he favoured 'free trade' but not free markets; he thought that personal liberty found its fullest expression (following Liberal idealist philosophers like T.H. Green and Bosanquet) in "service to the community"; and – provided it worked within a framework of law – he was not afraid of extending the powers of the state. He had a rather ambivalent relationship with the Labour Party, almost joining it in the 1900s and again in 1942, but was put off by the fact that it was "insufficiently socialist" (by which he meant too sentimental and populist, too weakly committed to an ethic of 'public service' and too much under the thumb of 'sectarian' trade unions). He was also frequently uncomplimentary about the Liberals, seeing them as full of "backwoodsmen" who could not face up to the structural economic realities of the 20th century. Nevertheless, he strongly favoured certain traditional Liberal principles, such as the rule of law, resistance to 'class interests', and the idea of the state (not as a tool of class interest), but as a unified 'impartial' mediator standing outside and above pluralistic 'society'. Though he loathed Stalinist tyranny, he was a reluctant admirer of late-1930s Soviet planning, particularly the way in which Soviet economists were using Hayekian price and wage theory as an instrument of full employment and manpower planning.

Beveridge and poverty

Although Beveridge had a lifelong commitment to the abolition of poverty, other reformers were sometimes shocked by his refusal to be sentimental about 'the poor'. He believed that the *causes* of poverty were primarily structural and environmental, but this did not mean that *solutions* to poverty could be divorced from considerations of incentives, rewards, civic and personal character. The poor were no less 'rational' than the rich, and like the rich would adjust their behaviour to get the most out of whatever was available. Society could have as many 'poor' as it liked, simply by paying people benefits solely on grounds of means, without any conditions about work or behaviour. This did not mean that Beveridge 'blamed' the poor for their poverty: on the contrary, he often surprised people by arguing that if claimants could get more from benefit than work then it was perfectly sensible (and for those with dependants even a moral duty) for them to do so. The 'fault' lay, not with claimants, but with defective public policies that stupidly deterred people from working or penalised saving (a fault exemplified in the Poor Law, and replicated by the various non-contributory and 'extended benefit' schemes of the 1920s and 1930s). The damage done by such policies was not so much economic and financial (they were often fiscally the cheapest alternative) but moral and civic, in that they generated a class of people who, even if they had the vote, were incapable of full citizenship and social participation. State policies should not 'infantilise' citizens by fostering dependence; instead they should aim primarily at preventing the *causes* of need, by providing skilled training, enforcing labour mobility, and encouraging foresight, independence and personal saving. Where *cash benefits* were necessary, they should be based on the principle of actively involving citizens in the management and surveillance of (state-subsidised, but not directly state-managed) contributory social insurance (as in the systems pioneered by friendly societies and skilled trade unions in the late-19th century).

The Beveridge Plan and its background

At the end of the 1930s it would have seemed wildly improbable that Beveridge would ever join the pantheon of great British social reformers. His ideas were very unpopular with many on the Labour 'Left', who were pressing at this time not for extended social insurance or organisation of manpower, but for unconditional 'work or maintenance'. When war broke out Beveridge initially saw 'social welfare' as having low priority. He hoped to be recalled to Whitehall to mobilise civilian labour, but his way was blocked by the hostility of Ernest Bevin, who viewed Beveridge as personally responsible for the state's curtailment of trade union liberties and privileges during the First World War. It was Bevin who in June 1941 got Beveridge shunted aside to the chairmanship of a technical committee on *Social insurance and allied services*. Beveridge literally wept with disappointment and dismay at this apparently marginal appointment; but over the next 18 months he came to see comprehensive social reform both as an essential element in boosting wartime morale, and as the clue to democratically-based post-war industrial reconstruction. The *Beveridge Plan* (1942), promising the slaying of the Five Giants of Want, Disease, Ignorance, Squalor and Idleness, was published to mass popular acclaim, and much political disgruntlement just after the victory at El Alamein in December 1942. Beveridge himself became a much-feted popular hero, and further shocked the inner circles of government by 'taking his show on the road' – appearing on hundreds of platforms and newsreels in Britain and America, and portraying full employment and social security, not merely as good in themselves, but as essential ingredients in the war against fascism and totalitarianism.

Principles of the Beveridge Plan

In fact, the war was an indispensable backcloth both to the underlying principles of the Beveridge Plan and to its wholly unexpected mass popularity. The Plan assumed a very high degree of social solidarity, a sense of 'everyone being in the same boat', that fitted the social reality of 1942 more than any earlier or later moment in British history. Many aspects of the Plan implicitly reflected the high degree of collective organisation and control over private resources that had become part of the familiar, taken-for-granted, climate of wartime. The detailed proposals of the Plan centred upon four key principles: full employment; universal family allowances; a comprehensive free national health service; and a unified flat-rate social insurance system for unemployment, sickness, disability, and pensions on retirement – all of which would cover all classes in the community. Many aspects of the Plan (though of course with many differences of detail) were to be carried through by government within a surprisingly short period – family allowances by the War coalition in 1944, social insurance, a national health service, and full employment policies by the Attlee government in 1946-48. For more than a decade thereafter it was widely assumed that poverty and unemployment had been abolished, and not until around 1960 did serious cracks begin to appear – with rising inflation, rising pressure on pensions' finance, revelations by social scientists about the persistence of poverty, rising benefit fraud, and – rather later – complaints from feminists that Beveridge had 'stereotyped' old-fashioned views of women as their husband's economic dependants. All these developments are in many ways unsurprising: history and society never stand still, and it was scarcely likely that what seemed like a 'social revolution' in the disciplined and austere 1940s would meet the demands and aspirations of the affluent, impatient and libertarian 1960s.

Beveridge and New Labour

It could, however, be argued that there were certain key principles and assumptions woven into the fabric of the Beveridge Plan that were too readily ignored or forgotten at the time, but which have a certain resonance – even an elective affinity – with some of the core ideas on New Labour. These may be summarised as follows:

- First there was the immensely detailed, cautious, and careful financial planning that Beveridge put into his 'Social Security Budget' (ie social spending in the early years was to add up to nothing more than the aggregate annual cost of public welfare schemes in the late-1930s, though spread more rationally; both individual contributions and the element of public subsidy were only to rise significantly *after* economic reconstruction).
- Only the 'national minimum' (ie benefits to cover subsistence) was to come via compulsory state insurance – additional benefits were to come from personal and mutual saving (preferably *not*, in Beveridge's view, via the commercial finance sector, but through self-governing partnerships within the state/voluntary sectors).
- Compulsory training or relocation was to be a standard part of the package for long-term unemployment.
- The National Health Service was to be not just for the treatment of 'sickness', but literally a means of 'servicing' post-war economic expansion by getting sick people back into the labour force as quickly as possible. (Beveridge assumed that in the long run health costs would *fall* as the nation became healthier.)
- 'Family allowances', payable in respect of all children, were specifically designed not just to relieve child poverty but to put an end to the pre-war anomaly that many poorer families were 'better off on the dole' than with a breadwinner in work.
- The linking of 'welfare' with 'citizenship', not in the legal but in the moral sense of the latter term: the whole package was premised on the principle that people would accept personal, familial and civic obligations in return for as-of-right benefits.
- The assumption that it was normal for all able-bodied adult persons of both sexes to be in the labour market (and a large proportion of disabled people as well). The only exceptions should be mothers looking after children and carers in the home. Beveridge spent more time wrestling with how to include mothers and carers within contributory insurance than on any other aspect of his report. He saw this as one of the most crucial dilemmas of citizen-based social security, and regarded his *failure* to solve it as the major structural weakness of his Plan.

References

Beveridge, W. (1909) *Unemployment: A problem of industry*, London: Longman.

Beveridge, Sir William (1942) *Social insurance and allied services* (Beveridge Report), Cmnd 6404, London: HMSO.

FOUR

Beveridge and the 21st century

Tony Atkinson

What William Beveridge would have proposed for a welfare state for the 21st century is hard to assess. He was a man of great complexity, driven by conflicting forces, which meant that his recommendations were far from consistent. His motives were often mixed: he supported family allowances both to help poor families and to keep down wages. The man who in 1938 warned that Britain could only compete in the world economy if it cut wages was the same person whose report in 1942 launched a crusade against the 'five giant evils' haunting Britain of 'Want, Disease, Ignorance, Squalor and Idleness', and whose 1944 Report on *Full employment in a free society* was prefaced with the saying that 'misery generates hate'. (These contrasts are highlighted in the Introduction to Harris' biography on Beveridge – Harris, 1977.)

One can be confident, however, that Beveridge's views would have evolved. He would be profoundly irritated by any assumption that his recommendations of 1942 would be just as applicable in 2002 or 2042. His own views changed frequently over time in response to changing problems and circumstances. This is well illustrated by the new Prologue to *Full employment in a free society* (Beveridge, 1960) written 16 years after the report appeared. In this new prologue of 1960 he was quite clear that the major problem facing Britain in the 1960s had become inflation, not unemployment. The issues had moved on, and his thinking moved on with them. He welcomed new problems and sought new solutions.

How might Beveridge have seen the challenges of the next century? Four suggestions are made here.

Social policy has to be integrated with economic policy

For Beveridge, the economic context was essential. He was not a person who saw economic and social policy as in distinct compartments. He would have deplored the trend of the post-war period to separate these two areas of policy making, with macro-economic policy being conducted on the assumption that any adverse consequences for poverty or social exclusion could be dealt with by an accommodating social policy. Beveridge was a 'joined-up' social scientist, who understood macro-economics as well as social administration. He would no doubt have welcomed today's involvement of the Treasury in anti-poverty policy, and the view that all aspects of government policy are relevant in the fight against social exclusion.

There are two aspects of the economic context which should be stressed. We have come full circle since Beveridge's 1960 Prologue, with unemployment having replaced inflation to become once again the main macro-economic concern. The unemployment rates he cited (1.1% in 1955) seem utopian today. Unlike the 1942 Beveridge Report, we can no longer assume that this can be achieved solely by macro-economic policy. There are interactions between employment and the welfare state. The welfare state for the 21st century has to be designed taking full account of its impact on the incentives for workers to work and for employers to employ people. At the same time, changes in the labour market cannot do it on their own: macro-economic policy still has an important influence on poverty and exclusion.

The second aspect is the transformation of the micro-economics of government policy. When Beveridge died, a large part of the economy was controlled by nationalised industries and there were substantial subsidies to private industry (for investment, regional policy etc). Today the government's main leverage is through regulation. One can see Beveridge if alive today volunteering to be head of the Strategic Rail Authority! He would do so because he would see this as the new source of influence and because he would understand that the issues were not simply economic but also social. In a society that is geographically highly mobile, the pricing policy of the train companies may be a major cause of the social exclusion of elderly people, dependant on public transport and unable to visit their children. If private savings are to be a major source of income in old age, then the regulation of financial intermediaries takes on wide social significance. Individual Savings Accounts (ISAs) are not just to encourage saving but also to prevent social exclusion in old age, and whether they are successful depends crucially on how they are regulated.

Social exclusion and investment in children

In re-reading his 1942 Report, Beveridge might well criticise himself for having held a too static conception of poverty. This is one of the main distinctions which is drawn today between poverty and social exclusion. People are socially excluded not just because they are currently without a job or income but because they have few prospects for the future. Assessment of the extent of social exclusion has therefore to go beyond current status.

This has led, in turn, to studies of poverty dynamics, which show that there is indeed turnover among low-income families. People recorded as poor at one particular date include those for whom it is a temporary experience of a year or so. But there are also many for whom poverty predominantly occurs in long spells, meaning that they have virtually no chance of escape. Concern about social exclusion tends to focus on the latter group, on the reasonable grounds that they are at risk of losing association with the mainstream of society, at least in terms of their standard of living.

However, temporary deprivation cannot be ignored in our thinking, particularly when we consider the impact on children. What may seem like a short period in an adult's life may be highly significant in terms of a child's education, development, and labour market entry. The child whose parent is off work may have a less adequate diet at a crucial stage in his or her growth; the decision whether or not to apply for university may come just when the father has been made redundant. The same applies to public provision. The child in whose early years hospitals have long waiting lists may have permanently reduced health status; children whose new school is postponed as a result of public expenditure cuts cannot relive their formative years.

All of this points to the importance of Child Benefit. Beveridge was early convinced of the case for distributing part of national income not as wages or profit but as family allowances. He introduced child allowances for the staff of the London School of Economics in 1924. In 1944, he said that "the worst feature of Want in Britain is its concentration upon children [which] represented a destruction of human capital" (Beveridge, 1960, p 255). In today's concern about social exclusion, it is precisely this lack of investment in our children that should be our focus. When we talk about people being socially excluded because they have few prospects for the future, we understand by 'prospects' not only their own but also those of their children. Child Benefit is a powerful commitment by a country to investment in its children.

Equally, it is important that there should be a child focus in other policy areas. One current example is the divorce between macro-economic indicators and the concerns of families. We talk about unemployment and inflation as though they were abstract economic constructions with validity in their own right, whereas they only make sense when related to the lives of individuals and their families. Price indices, for example, need to be related to what different types of family actually buy. We have made a start with pensioner price indices but a child-focused government would also have a price index which reflects the pattern of expenditure on goods and services for children. Equally, the statistics for unemployment treat individuals on their own, rather than living in families or households. In particular, the published unemployment rate tells us nothing about how far children are living in a household without an income from work. This points to the need to publish a statistic which shows the number of children in households adversely affected by unemployment: a 'child-focused unemployment rate'.

A new form for a national minimum

For Beveridge it would be inconceivable for Britain not to ensure a national minimum for all its citizens. Moreover, for all his changes of opinion, he remained convinced that this could not be guaranteed by means-tested social assistance. In his 1960 Prologue he deplored the continued dependence of pensioners on means-tested national assistance.

This does not mean that he would necessarily regard social insurance as the answer. He would not simply quote chapter and verse from *Social insurance and allied services* (Beveridge, 1942). He would recognise the many changes that had taken place in the family and the labour market. The social problems of today are not the same as those of the 1930s which motivated his 1942 recommendations.

As a radical, he might today look once again at the idea of a citizen's income, espoused by a number of leading Liberals in the 1940s, and now enjoying a revival of interest across Europe. Child Benefit is in a sense a citizen's income for children. But I suspect that he would hesitate about extending such a principle to adults on an unconditional basis. Just as he saw unemployment insurance as inextricably linked with unemployment exchanges, so today he might see a citizen's income as inextricably linked with a condition of reciprocity. Entitlement to the citizen's income would carry with it the obligation of the citizen to participate in socially recognised activities. The conditions for such a 'participation income' could be broadly defined, including work as an employee or self-employed, absence from work on grounds of sickness, being unemployed but available for work, engaging in approved forms of education or training, and caring for young, elderly or disabled dependants. As the last examples make clear, the condition is not *paid* work; it is a wider definition of social contribution.

Such a scheme would in many respects be a natural development of Welfare to Work. Just as society accepts an obligation to develop socially inclusive policies and institutions, so individuals would be expected to accept an obligation to participate.

The welfare state has to be seen in an international context

Beveridge was international in his outlook. He toured Germany to learn about their labour exchanges in 1907; the Beveridge Report made extensive references to social insurance in other countries. As already noted, he was concerned about the competitiveness of British industry in a world economy.

Today he would doubtless recognise Britain's exposure to the forces of the world economy, although he might point out that in this respect we have come full circle, the economy being no more open than when he began his career at the start of the century. I am not sure, however, that he would conclude from this that national governments are powerless, nor that globalisation has rendered meaningless the concept of the national welfare state. It is not the case that all countries are driven by economic imperatives to follow a particular line. The attempt by bodies such as the International Monetary Fund or Organisation for Economic Cooperation and Development to impose a particular approach based on labour market flexibility and dismantling of social protection is not justified by appealing to economics. It involves a political judgement as well.

At the same time, he would recognise that Britain's membership of the European Union is an important consideration in the design of the welfare state. Social policy remains a national prerogative, so that it does not directly constrain the British government. But Europe is an opportunity, an opportunity to shift policy in the desired direction. Two examples follow from the earlier discussion. First, Britain could promote the integration of social and economic policy. This affects not just macro-economic policy but also micro-economic policy, notably in the field of regulation. Second, the stress on Child Benefit could be given further impetus if Europe as a whole were to agree on a European minimum level of Child Benefit, mandated on member states. 'Investing in Europe's children' would be an attractive rallying call for the 21st century.

References

Beveridge, Sir William (1942) *Social insurance and allied services* (Beveridge Report), Cmnd 6404, London: HMSO.

Beveridge, W. (1960) *Full employment in a free society*, London: Allen and Unwin.

Harris, J. (1977) *William Beveridge: A biography*, Oxford: Clarendon Press.

FIVE

Beveridge and New Labour: poverty then and now

John Hills

Beveridge and the causes of 'Want'

In his famous 1942 Report, *Social insurance and allied services*, Sir William Beveridge set out his plans for social security after the end of the War:

> **The plan for Social Security ... starts from a diagnosis of want – of the circumstances in which, in the years just preceding the present war, families and individuals in Britain might lack the means of healthy subsistence. (Beveridge, 1942, para 11)**

The evidence he used was drawn from a number of pre-war surveys in particular towns, especially the work of Seebohm Rowntree in his surveys of York in both 1936 and one hundred years ago in 1899.

The key conclusion Beveridge drew from these surveys was that the principal causes of 'Want' could be divided between 'interruption or loss of earning power' – accounting for three quarters to five sixths of the total – and the effects of large family size – accounting for 'practically the whole' of the rest (Beveridge, 1942).

In Rowntree's 1899 survey more than half of the 'primary poverty'[1] was due to low wages. Only 18% was due to unemployment or death of the main wage earner. By contrast, in 1936, unemployment, old age and other causes which could be met by social insurance accounted for five sixths of the total, and large families for another 8%. Low wages only accounted for a tenth of the total (figures from Evans and Glennerster, 1993, Figure 1).

These observations led directly to Beveridge's recommendations: a comprehensive system of unemployment benefits, old age pensions, widows' benefits, and disability benefits, all based on insurance rights earned during the good parts of people's working lives. But his prescription was not only about cash benefits. Straying way beyond the brief which had been set for his committee, he argued that his plan for social security was based on three 'assumptions', themselves major foundations of post-war social and economic policies:

- children's allowances (today's Child Benefit), to cope with the problems of large families;
- comprehensive health and rehabilitation services (which became the NHS);
- commitment to avoidance of mass unemployment. (Beveridge, 1942, para 14).

Nor was his concern only with poverty in the sense of lack of income:

> **Income security which is all that can be given by social insurance is so inadequate a provision for human happiness that to put it forward by itself as a sole or principal measure of reconstruction hardly seems worth doing. It should be accompanied by an announced determination to use the powers of the state to whatever extent may prove necessary to ensure for all, not indeed absolute continuity of work, but a reasonable chance of productive employment. (Beveridge, 1942, para 440)[2]**

Defining poverty

In arguing that the proposals in his 1942 Report could lead to 'the abolition of Want', Beveridge drew heavily on the work of Seebohm Rowntree and others in defining a poverty line in order to assess the numbers living in poverty. However, the use he made of Rowntree's research to argue that his proposed benefit levels, constrained by available resources, *would* achieve 'healthy subsistence' is controversial (Veit-Wilson, 1994); the actual benefit rates set post-war did not fully reflect inflation during the War (Abel-Smith, 1994); and his proposals failed to cope with 'the problem of rent' – widely varying housing costs between and across regions (Glennerster and Evans, 1994)[3].

His use of Rowntree's work is controversial because Rowntree effectively measured poverty according to two standards. To give the overall numbers living in poverty he used standards which clearly related to the prevailing standard of living of the country. For his 1899 survey his total count for the proportion of York's population living in poverty

(28%) was based on the subjective measure of 'living in obvious want and squalor'. He also calculated a 'primary poverty' line based on families having too little income 'to obtain the minimum necessaries for the maintenance of merely physical efficiency', however efficiently they husbanded their resources and avoided any other kind of spending.

In his 1936 survey, Beveridge's key source, Rowntree, again used two scales. This time his overall measure of poverty was based on a more scientific measure of the income required to meet the 'Human Needs of Labour'. This standard represented the minimum necessary not just for physical efficiency but for 'a healthy life', including items seen as essential in the social circumstances of the 1930s, such as a bath, which had not been in the 1890s (Atkinson, 1989). He also calculated that the proportion of York's population falling below the 1899 'primary poverty' line adjusted for inflation had fallen from 10 to 4%. It was only against this minimal standard that Beveridge could reach the conclusion that interruption of earnings (unemployment, illness, old age) was the main cause of poverty. Against Rowntree's higher standard, low wages still accounted for a third of poverty (Roll, 1992).

It was also only by taking a standard which was little better than Rowntree's primary poverty line that Beveridge could argue that his proposed social insurance benefit levels would 'abolish Want'. They were not high enough to meet the 'Human Needs of Labour' standard which Rowntree argued was required to cover all 'essentials' in the Britain of the 1930s.

This question of what is deemed 'essential' runs through all attempts to define poverty standards. Our ideas of what is essential change over time. Back in 1776 Adam Smith famously argued that,

> **By necessaries, I understand not only the commodities which are indispensably necessary for the support of life but whatever the custom of the country renders it indecent for creditable people, even of the lowest order, to be without ... in the present time a creditable day labourer would be ashamed to appear in public without a linen shirt. (Smith, 1776, p 691 in 1982 edn, quoted in Alcock, 1997)**

A century later, Rowntree's 1899 investigators in York had their own standards of what constituted 'obvious want and squalor'. By 1936 Rowntree was including not just a bath, but also beer and newspapers. Thirty years ago, Professor Peter Townsend developed his measure of poverty in terms of deprivation, where people lacked "the resources to obtain the types of diet, participate in the activities and have the living conditions and amenities which are customary, or at least widely encouraged or approved, in the societies to which they belong" (Townsend, 1979, p 31). Assessing deprivation in 1968/69 he included not just a bath and other standard amenities, but also a refrigerator and a week's holiday away from home (Townsend, 1979, Table 6.3).

The problem with all this is the question of who decides what *is* essential for participation in their own society. Is a telephone essential today? Is a television? Here television itself helps, through the *Breadline Britain* surveys commissioned by London Weekend Television in 1983 and 1990. They asked a sample of the population as a whole – not just 'experts' – what they thought were 'necessities'. In 1983 the majority did not think a telephone was a necessity. By 1990, 56% did (Gordon and Pantazis, 1997, Table 3.1). On the other hand, few regarded a home computer as a necessity.

According to the 1990 *Breadline Britain* survey, 20% of the population lacked three or more 'necessities' identified by the majority of the population (up from 14% in 1983). At the same time 21% of the population (not necessarily the same ones) had less than half contemporary average income according to the Department of Social Security's *Households Below Average Income* analysis (before housing costs), up from 8% in 1979.

In the future, what are seen as necessities will change again. It is not just that as a society our standards change as we become more affluent; it is also that what is needed to give people what last year's Nobel prize winner Professor Amartya Sen calls 'capabilities' depend on contemporary society (see, for example, Sen, 1992). 'Appearing in public without shame' now needs more than Adam Smith's linen shirt. Rowntree would not have regarded a telephone or a driving licence as needed in order to find a job. Today they can be essential. Tomorrow, finding work may be hard without access to the internet. Parents are prepared to make huge sacrifices to stop their children from being left out or standing out at school. Twenty years ago football strips and the right trainers were not an issue. Today they are (Middleton et al, 1994). Rising living standards in general can make life harder for those on an income which is fixed, even allowing for inflation.

And participation in society – or exclusion from it – is not just about cash, as Beveridge recognised in his identification of the other 'giants on the path to reconstruction' – not just Want, but also Disease, Ignorance, Squalor, and Idleness (Beveridge, 1942, para 8).

How the world has changed since Beveridge

Beveridge's plan for the 'abolition of Want' was based on his reading of research on the nature of poverty and society in the 1930s. But the country has changed in the last 60 years.

First, and most strikingly, the position of women has changed massively from that assumed by Beveridge. He drew on the 1931 Census to argue that "more than seven out of eight of all housewives, that is to say married women of working age, made marriage their sole occupation; less than one in eight of all housewives was also gainfully occupied" (Beveridge, 1942, para 108). He assumed that after the War the position would return to this. He made social insurance rights for married women dependent on their husband's employment record:

> **… all women by marriage acquire a new economic and social status, with risks and rights different from those of the unmarried. (Beveridge, 1942, para 108)**

The biggest of these risks – apart from interruption of husbands' earnings – was widowhood. Coping with a society in which 23% of all families with dependent children were headed by a lone parent (only 1% accounted for by widowhood – 1995 figures from General Household Survey) would have been hard for Beveridge to comprehend.

Second, our society has aged. This would have surprised him less. In fact, he did not foresee the post-war baby-boom and assessed his plans against a projection that nearly 21% of the population would already be over state pension age as early as 1971 (Beveridge, 1942, Table XI). In fact, only 18% were over pension age as late as 1991, and the projections do not reach 21% until 2021 (ONS, 1996). Nonetheless, the pattern is very different from the pre-war period on which Beveridge focused, with only 10% over state pension age in 1931. This not only puts more strain on public and private pension schemes, but also on the 'comprehensive health services' which he 'assumed'. And the forecast increase, particularly in the numbers of the very elderly, forms the background to the report and recommendations of the recent Royal Commission on Long Term Care for the Elderly.

Compounding this on the social security side has been the growth of 'early retirement'. Employment rates among men aged over 50 have dropped dramatically in the last 20 years: 800,000 fewer men aged 50-65 were in paid work in 1997 than would have been at 1979 employment rates. Two fifths of men aged 55-65 are not in paid work now, compared to one fifth 20 years ago (Campbell, 1999). Women in their fifties have not increased their labour force participation in the same way as younger women.

Third, the labour market has changed. The technological revolution of the last 25 years and the effect of economic globalisation have decisively changed the position of people with no or few qualifications and of less skilled workers in general. After the mid-1970s the pattern of wage relativities – previously changing little since the last century – changed dramatically, with little growth in real hourly pay for the low paid between 1975 and 1993, while high pay grew by more than half (Gosling et al, 1998, Figure 1.1: Family Expenditure Survey data figures refer to 10th and 90th percentiles of real male hourly wage). The overall level of income inequality rose between the late 1970s and early 1990s to rates not seen for the previous 40 years (Hills, 1995, Figure 12).

Fourth, the situation is different because the post-war role of the state has been very different, not least because of the kinds of changes in social security and the welfare state set in train by Beveridge and the Attlee government, but also as a result of continued evolution since then to meet new needs, and sometimes new constraints. In many ways this provides the kind of social underpinning and income security which Beveridge was arguing for. In others, the way in which the state tries to do this can have undesirable side-effects.

Finally, whatever our problems, we are a far more affluent society. This expands the opportunities available to us, but it also increases pressures. Aspirations are higher for social services as well as private ones. What people see as an acceptable, or rather, unacceptably low, standard of living is affected by the standard of living of those around them, with the individual and economic pressures which this creates.

Nine features of poverty today

All of these changes have affected the nature of poverty today in ways which are crucial to thinking about the best ways of combating it. The figures quoted below relate to those with relatively low incomes; other measures of 'poverty' might give a somewhat different picture, but most features would remain the same.

First, *low incomes of those in work* are a bigger factor than Beveridge planned for. A third of the poorest fifth of the population in 1996/97 had income from employment (DSS, 1998a, Table D2: Family Resources Survey-based figures for distribution before housing costs, including self-employed).

Second, formal unemployment is not the only cause of *non-employment*: 17% of the poorest fifth had an unemployed head or spouse in 1996/97, but another 25% fell into the Department of Social Security's 'other' category of non-employment for those aged under 60 – not working because of long-term sickness or disability, early retirement or lone parenthood (DSS, 1998a, Table D2).

Third, *lone parents and their children* make up a sixth of the poorest fifth, twice their overall representation in the population as a whole (DSS, 1998a, Table D1). Evidence from surveys which follow the same people from year to year shows that lone parents (usually women) and their children are the group most likely to be persistently poor – three times as likely as the population as a whole to be in the poorest 30% for six years in a row, and with more than half of them in the bottom 30% for at least four years out of six (including the first) (DSS, 1998a, Table 4.6: DSS analysis of British Household Panel Survey data).

Fourth, *children* as a whole are over-represented among those in households with low incomes. Almost three children in ten are in households in the poorest fifth (DSS, 1998a, p 1). The proportion of children in households with less than half the average income (adjusted for family size) rose from about one in ten in the 1970s to well over one in four in the early 1990s (Gregg et al, 1999: Family Expenditure Survey-based figures for equivalised income before housing costs). Although children come from families with low incomes, their parents may go to great lengths to spend enough to allow them to fit in with the children around them. But the implication of this is that parents – particularly mothers – are going without to try to protect them (Middleton et al, 1997).

Nonetheless, recent research looking at what has happened to all of the children born in one week in March 1958 shows that childhood experiences of poverty seem to have effects lasting well into adult life. Even allowing for the effects of a wide range of other influences, indications of childhood poverty were linked to 15 out of 19 unfavourable adult outcomes. Children with parents reporting financial difficulties or receiving free school meals at 7, 11 and 16 were 2½ times as likely to have no qualifications by age 33. Boys whose families were poor had their chances of degree-level qualifications reduced by three quarters (*after* allowing for things like educational test scores when children) (Hobcraft, 1998).

Other analysis of the same survey shows a chain linking childhood poverty to reduced rates of staying on at school after 16, increased chances of contact with the police, and on to higher risks of low wages and unemployment at 23 and 33. Fathers' earnings by themselves predict half of the variation in their children's earnings at age 33 (Gregg et al, 1999).

Fifth, *qualifications* have a crucial influence both in links between generations and persistent low income. The evidence on persistent low income suggests that only about 5% of adults with degrees have incomes in the poorest 30% for at least four out of six years, but 32% of those with no qualifications (DSS, 1998a, Table 4.6: based on Department of Social Security analysis of British Household Panel Survey).

Sixth, Britain has become a multi-racial society, but particular *ethnic minorities* are hugely over-represented among those with low incomes. Seven out of ten households with a Pakistani or Bangladeshi head were in the poorest fifth in 1996/97 and three out of ten of those with a 'black' or Indian head (DSS, 1998a, Table 2.6: Family Resources Survey definitions of ethnic groups; figures for income before housing costs). In the 1991 Census, more than half of the Bangladeshi population was living in the tenth of wards which were ranked as the most deprived nationally (Green, 1996).

Seventh, *pensioners* are still over-represented among those with low incomes, although less so than in the past. Single pensioners, many of them women, are particularly likely to have persistently low incomes: nearly a quarter of those with low incomes six years in a row in the early 1990s were single pensioners, three times their overall proportion of the population (DSS, 1998a, Table 4.8). With lone mothers also affected by persistent poverty, adult *women* as a whole made up 47% of those with persistently low incomes in the 1990s, against only 41% of the whole population (DSS, 1998a, Table 4.8).

Eighth, *housing tenure* has become a strong predictor of low income. Councils and housing associations are increasingly housing only the poor: by 1994/95 75% of those in social housing were in the poorest two fifths, and only 16% in the top half (Hills, 1998a, Figure 9: based on Department of Social Security analysis of 1994/95 and 1995/96 Family Expenditure Survey, including self-employed and before housing costs). Tenants of social housing were four times more likely than owner-occupiers to have persistently low incomes between 1991 and 1996 (DSS, 1998a, Table 4.6: based on British Household Panel Survey; the ratio is the same on both definitions of 'persistence').

Finally, geography matters and compounds the problems for those living in *low-income neighbourhoods*. Areas vary on a huge variety of indicators. Two examples: the poorest 284 wards in England and Wales in 1991 had nearly half (45%) of their working-age population not working, studying or training, compared to an average of 24% for England and Wales as a whole. Thirty-eight per cent of their population were 'deprived' on a composite measure from Census questions, compared to a national average of 18% (Power, 1999, Table 1)[4].

New Labour and poverty

In its first two years in office, the new government can point to a widening patchwork of measures aimed at many of the multiple drivers of increased relative poverty and social exclusion[5]:

- *The work agenda:* not just the New Deal, and Working Families Tax Credit, but also the policies aimed at macro-economic stability. As for Beveridge, overall employment levels are central.
- *Health:* protection of the NHS, including new resources; the health inequality agenda (including the Acheson Report and White Paper to come). Again this echoes the centrality of 'comprehensive health services' as an assumption for Beveridge.
- *Children:* increases in Child Benefit; higher Income Support for younger children; the greater generosity of the Working Families Tax Credit than Family Credit; childcare and under-fives strategies, including Sure Start (echoing Beveridge and the 'assumption' of children's allowances).
- *Education / skills:* extra resources for education, training, focus on school standards.
- *Low income in work:* the minimum wage; the Working Families Tax Credit; and reforms to National Insurance Contributions lowering them for the low paid.
- *A shift in the general tax burden from those with low incomes:* reduced VAT on fuel; the National Insurance Contribution reforms; and the 10p starting income tax rate.
- *Pensioners:* a real increase in pensioner Income Support (renamed the Minimum Income Guarantee), with partial commitment to future earnings-linking under the pension reform proposals (DSS, 1998b), the new State Second Pension will be more generous to the lower paid and carers than the State Earnings Related Pension Scheme it replaces.
- *Low-income areas:* the work of the Social Exclusion Unit in general and follow-up to its report on low-income neighbourhoods in particular (Social Exclusion Unit, 1998); the New Deal for Communities; increased capital for council housing repairs; Employment, Education and Health Action Zones.

This 'patchwork' does, however, have some holes in it:

- The government's rhetoric often sounds as if Welfare to Work measures will completely transform the numbers on benefits, rather than what is more likely, having positive and useful *net* effects for only a relatively small percentage of beneficiaries (see Gardiner, 1997, for discussion of the effects of such schemes before 1997). This means that there will still be many of working age dependent on state benefits.
- Overall policy is for continued price-linking of benefits with exceptions (so far) for Income Support for younger children, Child Benefit, and low-income pensioners. This implies a continuing fall in relative living standards for others remaining on benefit. Of course, the government's priority is to move people *off* benefit and so reduce the *numbers* on low incomes. Nonetheless, those who remain will fall further behind.
- For most lone parents the increases in Child Benefit and Income Support for younger children and the Working Families Tax Credit compensate for the effects of abolition of lone-parent additions (producing 'equalisation up' in the treatment of one- and two-parent families), but this still leaves little *improvement* for this large low-income group (with high levels of persistent low income).
- The strategy for the very poorest pensioners is to encourage greater take-up of the means-tested Minimum Income Guarantee. However, lack of complete take-up is a long-standing problem; it remains to be seen how successful new measures will be.
- As it is described in the Green Paper on pensions, the new State Second Pension does not fully achieve the government's aim of getting (single) people with a full working life clear of an earnings-linked Minimum Income Guarantee (Rake et al, 1999). The Green Paper's calculations suggest that its proposals would leave public spending on pensions in 2050 well below today's share of national income. This leaves headroom to make the second pension more generous without higher spending in the long run than today, increasing the chances of pensioners getting clear of means-testing.

However, the commitment to an annual official 'poverty audit' starting this year will highlight such gaps, and will – once data for the next two years are available – give an opportunity to identify groups which had not been affected by measures taken to far. Its findings could then be used to adjust or to add to policy accordingly to ensure that the government's overall aim of "raising the living standards of the poorest" (Tony Blair, interviewed by the *Independent*, 29 July 1996) was met.

Notes

[1] 'Primary poverty' for Rowntree was an income so low that it would be impossible, however efficiently money was managed, to reach the most austere subsistence level. Nearly 10% of York's 1899 population had incomes below this. In all, Rowntree found 28% of York's population then in poverty, that is, living in conditions of 'obvious want and squalor' according to his investigators.

[2] Other aspects of Beveridge's thought at the time were rather less 'New Labour' – see Jose Harris' chapter in Hills et al (1994).

[3] 'The problem of rent' continues, so far, to defeat government attempts to reform the structure of Housing Benefit.

[4] 'Poorest wards' are those in the bottom 5% in the 1991 Census on *both* worklessness and deprivation using the 'Breadline Britain index'.

[5] For more detailed discussion of measures in the first 15 months, see Hills (1998b); for recent trends in income distribution see Hills (1998a).

References

Abel-Smith, B. (1994) 'The Beveridge Report: its origins and outcomes', in J. Hills, J. Ditch and H. Glennerster (eds) *Beveridge and social security*, Oxford: Clarendon Press, pp 10-12.

Alcock, P. (1997) *Understanding poverty*, Basingstoke: Macmillan.

Atkinson, A.B. (1989) 'Poverty in Britain from the 1930s to the 1980s', in A.B. Atkinson, *Poverty and social security*, Hemel Hempstead: Harvester, pp 40-61.

Beveridge, Sir William (1942) *Social insurance and allied services*, Cmnd 6404, London: HMSO.

Campbell, N. (1999) *The decline of employment among older people in Britain*, CASE Paper 19, London: London School of Economics.

DSS (Department of Social Security) (1998a) *Households Below Average Income*, London: DSS.

DSS (1998b) *A new contract for welfare: Partnership in pensions*, Cm 4179, London: The Stationery Office.

Evans, M. and Glennerster, H. (1993) *Squaring the circle? The inconsistencies and constraints of Beveridge's plans*, Welfare State Programme Discussion Paper No 86, London: London School of Economics.

Gardiner, K. (1997) *Bridges from benefit to work: A review*, York: Joseph Rowntree Foundation.

Glennerster, H. and Evans, M. (1994) 'Beveridge and his assumptive worlds: the incompatibilities of a flawed design', in J. Hills, J. Ditch and H. Glennerster (eds) *Beveridge and social security*, Oxford: Clarendon Press, pp 56-72.

Gordon, D. and Pantazis, C. (1997) *Breadline Britain in the 1990s*, Aldershot: Ashgate.

Gosling, A., Machin, S. and Meghir, C. (1998) *The changing distribution of male wages in the UK*, IFS Working Paper 98/9, London: Institute of Fiscal Studies.

Green, A. (1996) *The geography of poverty and wealth*, Warwick: Institute for Employment Research, University of Warwick.

Gregg, P., Harkness, A. and Machin, S. (1999) *Child development and family income*, York: Joseph Rowntree Foundation.

Hills, J. (1995) *Income and wealth, Volume 2: A summary of the evidence*, York: Joseph Rowntree Foundation.

Hills, J. (1998a) *Income and wealth: The latest evidence*, York: Joseph Rowntree Foundation.

Hills, J. (1998b) *Thatcherism, New Labour and the welfare state*, CASE Paper 13, London: London School of Economics.

Hills, J., Ditch, J. and Glennerster, H. (eds) (1994) *Beveridge and social security*, Oxford: Clarendon Press.

Hobcraft, J. (1998) *Intergenerational and life-course transmission of social exclusion*, CASE Paper 15, London: London School of Economics.

Middleton, S., Ashworth, K. and Walker, R. (1994) *Family fortunes: Pressures on parents and children in the 1990s*, London: CPAG.

Middleton, S., Ashworth, K. and Braithwaite, I. (1998) *Small fortunes: Spending on children, childhood poverty and parental sacrifice*, York: Joseph Rowntree Foundation.

ONS (Office for National Statistics) (1996) *National Population Projections*, Series PP2, No 20, GB figures.

Power, A. (1999) 'Area problems and multiple deprivation', Contribution to Treasury/CASE seminar on *Persistent poverty and lifetime inequality*, CASE Report 5, London: London School of Economics.

Rake, K., Falkingham, J. and Evans, M. (1999) *Tightropes and tripwires: New Labour's proposals and means-testing in old age*, CASE Paper 23, London: London School of Economics.

Roll, J. (1992) *Understanding poverty*, London: Family Policy Studies Centre.

Sen, A. (1992) *Inequality re-examined*, Oxford: Clarendon Press.

Social Exclusion Unit (1998) *Bringing Britain together*, London: The Stationery Office.

Townsend, P. (1979) *Poverty in the United Kingdom*, Harmondsworth: Penguin.

Veit-Wilson, J. (1994) 'Condemned to deprivation: Beveridge's responsibility for the invisibility of poverty', in J. Hills, J. Ditch and H. Glennerster (eds) *Beveridge and social security*, Oxford: Clarendon Press, pp 97-117.

B Modern social justice

SIX

Notes on social justice and the welfare state

Anthony Giddens

1 Social justice remains a fundamental concern of any Left of Centre party today – it is one of the main things that defines it as such. Make no bones about it, social justice involves redistribution, the reduction of inequalities. New Labour must embrace a redistributive project, just as Old Labour did.

2 The reasons for this are both ethical and deeply practical. Ethical, because we are all citizens of the same political community, sharing a common identity. Practical, because the very integrity and continuity of a society is threatened if inequalities grow too large. Many social ills come from extreme inequalities – high levels of crime, the deterioration of neighbourhoods, lowered life expectancy etc.

3 Old style redistribution – tax and spend – is not the best way to tackle inequalities today. This is because:

- Most went on welfare state spending. The welfare state, however, was never as effective at redistribution as it might have been – many studies show this.
- There is no longer a large working class needing to be brought into the wider society. Less than 20% of the working population are now in blue-collar work. There is now a much larger and diversified middle class.
- It makes sense to define inequality as exclusion, because there are some 10-15% at the bottom economically, and spatially, excluded from the position of the majority.
- People live freer and more open lives than they used to do – heavy-handed collectivism is a thing of the past.

4 Redistribution should be redefined as the redistribution of life chances – providing the possibilities for individuals to realise their potential.

Hence the centrality of education, and active labour market policy. There is also a need to deal with the problems associated with the welfare state itself – for example, the fact that benefits can frustrate the very aims they were supposed to achieve.

5   However, social justice can never be defined only in terms of equality of opportunity, or only in relation to the labour market. At any one time there are many people outside the labour market and government has an obligation to protect the vulnerable. Redistribution of life chances here means creating the means of living a decent life – not just adequate personal resources, but community renewal, provision of local services and reducing crime.

6   Social justice can therefore never be wholly separated from security – which it was the main aim of Beveridge's welfare state to provide. The welfare state was essentially an insurance or risk management system – the need now is for a quite different balance of risk and security.

7   People often say that inequality is more or less everywhere on the increase and that nothing much can be done about it. Neither claim is correct. Inequalities are in some contexts becoming reduced – the most obvious and important case is inequalities between men and women. Inequalities, at least as usually measured, have gone down in some countries. Those countries that have followed the most extreme free market policies have the largest economic inequalities.

8   Some notes on Beveridge.
•   At age 80, he said: "I am still radical and young enough to believe that mountains can be moved".
•   In drawing up his famous Plan, Beveridge constantly stressed that a good social policy should at all costs avoid a 'Santa Claus State', in which people would expect 'something for nothing'.
•   As early as 1962, the celebrated theorist of the welfare state, T.H. Marshall, stressed that the Beveridge system was the 'child of austerity'.
•   Beveridge's 'five giants on the road to reconstruction' were Want, Ignorance, Squalor, Idleness and Disease. A lot of progress has been made since those days when Beveridge's giants were all negatives. Policy goals should be positive – Autonomy, Active Health, Education, Well-being and Initiative.
•   Beveridge himself came to loathe the term 'welfare state'.
•   Beveridge was Director of the London School of Economics from 1919 to 1937.

9 It is important to address social exclusion 'at the top'. We do not want a society with impoverished public services so that anyone who has got a bit of money opts out of them into a ghetto of private schools, medicine, housing etc. There are many ways of coping with this issue – for example, by promoting a culture of responsible capitalism, by increased development of not-for-profit organisations providing high quality services, through public–private partnerships, and by an emphasis upon reforming and modernising public sector institutions rather than simply flinging money at them.

10 Finally, there is the European Union and growing inequalities on a world scale. An important element in tackling these issues is the effort to secure a new framework for global economic institutions. Getting a more stable currency regime and helping investment flow to the areas that need it would help with everyone's problems.

SEVEN

Social justice

Raymond Plant

Context

It might be useful to situate this Lecture initially in Beveridge's own context. The Prime Minister has been anxious to unite again the tradition of 'Social' or 'New' Liberalism and Social Democracy. Beveridge was a New Liberal[1] – so what did this imply? Well one thing that it implied was a concern for social justice and a rejection of endorsement of untrammelled market forces characteristic of classical liberalism. New Liberal politics in the late Victorian and early Edwardian era rejected the view of the free market economy and the 'night watchman' state of classical liberal theory. Central to this change was that they adopted a more complex view of freedom than did classical liberals. Classical liberals believed that freedom was *negative*: the absence of intentional coercion – it did not imply the possession or resources and opportunities. The role of the state was to enforce contracts and mutual non-interference. New Liberals (eg T.H. Green, Sir H. Jones, Asquith, Haldane, Lloyd George) believed that negative liberty was not enough – there had to be positive freedom – that is to say, access to resources, opportunities and income that would make all into genuine citizens. The *locus classicus* of the argument is in T.H. Green's essay 'Liberal legislation and freedom of contract' (Green, 1888). On the classical liberal view justice was essentially procedural: the maintenance of the rules of society guaranteeing mutual non-interference (given this restricted view of freedom). For the New Liberal the role of the state was also to secure to individuals the general resources of opportunities needed for freedom in the now more extended sense of the word. So for the New Liberals, of whom Beveridge was one, part of the argument for a greater role for the state was rooted in a different conception of freedom once this became embodied in New Liberal legislation, for example, the Ground Game Act, the Irish Land Bill and culminating in the old age pension legislation of the Asquith government. Such was the change of intellectual environment from classical to New Liberalism. Gladstone, whose roots were in classical liberalism, said in a letter that he was "fundamentally a dead man, fundamentally a Peel and Cobden man" (a dead man because classical liberalism in relation to the economy of the sort advocated by Peel and Cobden had been overtaken by New or Social Liberalism). At the same time, while the New Liberals wanted to see a role for the state in securing positive freedom, they also insisted upon two interrelated things. The first was that the provision of the resources for positive freedom should not undermine personal responsibility – a very strong theme, for example, in Arnold Toynbee's writings; second, that local voluntary institutions such as Toynbee Hall could be used in a way to help the poor develop a greater degree of responsibility. This was to be achieved partly by education in the life skills and partly by the force of example on the part of those working in such places.

This change in the intellectual climate within Liberalism which has a profound influence on Beveridge also meshed in with the growth of Social Democratic ideas. Social Democracy has its origin in Germany with Ferdinand Lasalle and in the next generation E. Bernstein, who lived in London and was involved with the Fabians. Social Democrats, in sharp contrast to Marxists, believed that it was possible to manipulate a market order and private ownership by political means so that both were able to be used to serve more socially just ends. (Marx, 1996, had criticised this view in *A critique of the Gotha Programme*.) So, Social Democratic ideas about securing greater social justice through political means meshed in a good deal with changes in the intellectual context of Liberals. Of course, these two movements in the UK split apart for all sorts of reasons. If the Social Democratic and the New Liberal tradition can be reunited, it is going to be through agreed ideas about social justice as much, if not more, than anything else.

The critique of social justice

So how are we to understand social justice today? One major point which relates to all of the above is that the 1970s onwards saw quite a revival of classical liberal ideas about freedom and the market. Think tanks such as the Institute of Economic Affairs, the Adam Smith Institute, the Centre for Policy Studies, the Social Market Foundation, provided outlets for essentially classical liberal diagnoses and prescriptions. Equally, major economic thinkers such as Buchanan, Friedman and Hayek (all Nobel prize winners) wrote penetrating critiques of the ideas of social justice. These critiques were turned to political advantage by Margaret Thatcher, Keith Joseph, Geoffrey Howe etc. I still think that this critique has to be confronted. I don't think that it can be dismissed as an outmoded 1980s agenda because there are still powerful voices which argue that globalisation will necessarily lead to minimal government and the most extensive market economy possible – essentially the thesis that globalisation entails economic liberalism and the abandonment of social justice.

The moral arguments deployed by economic liberals against the idea of social justice (which Hayek regarded as a 'mirage', to use the title of one of his books) are as follows:

- The Social Liberals/Social Democrats are wrong to believe that freedom is linked to ability, thus to resources and opportunities. The argument here is that freedom and ability are logically distinct. No one is able to do all that he/she is free to do. However rich or talented I am, I can only do a small number of all the things that I am free to do. Hence, freedom and ability must be separated. Freedom is mutual non-interference; it is not about social justice, that is to say, using government to secure individuals' resources and opportunities. Sir Keith Joseph put this point well when he said in *Equality*: "poverty is not unfreedom" (Joseph and Sumption, 1979). Freedom is negative: about mutual non-interference; not positive about the possession of resources.

- It is argued that injustice can only be caused by intentional action. The outcomes of economic markets which make some rich and some poor are not intended. They are, rather, the unintended outcome of millions of individual acts of buying and selling. Since the overall outcome, the so-called 'distribution' of income and wealth is not intended, it is not unjust.

- We have a diverse and pluralistic society and it is not possible in such a society to secure agreement on distributive criteria. Goods/ services/income/wealth could be distributed according to all sorts of criteria: need, equality (and if equality, equality of opportunity or equality of outcome), desert, contribution etc. Distribution according to one or the other would produce very different outcomes. How are we to arrive at agreement about these basic distributive criteria? We cannot, and hence we should abandon the idea of social justice as a guide to policy.

- In the view of economic liberal critics the lack of moral agreement on criteria of social justice will have dire political consequences. If the government takes on a distributive role, all sorts of groups in society will seek resources for the interests that they represent while at the same time the government will not have, and cannot have, a clear set of consensual moral principles to guide its distributive decisions. In the circumstances, distributive politics will be turned into a vicious kind of zero-sum interest group politics in which the government will fall victim to coalitions of the strongest interest groups (such a critique is a recurring theme of Sam Brittan's books and journalism). Far from social justice being a noble ideal, it becomes a rhetorical fig leaf for interest group politics when distributive politics is pursued in an ethical vacuum.

- The fifth element in the critique has to do with what might be called the public administration consequences of social justice. If the government takes on a distributive role, it is argued, this will mean two related things. On the one hand, a growth of bureaucracy charged with carrying out distributive decisions. On the other hand, it will mean that because we lack detailed moral agreement about principles of social justice, a very great deal of discretionary power is going to have to be placed in the hands of bureaucrats. The reason for this is that we cannot write detailed rules to guide detailed distributive policies (Hayek) and in these circumstances bureaucrats have to be given discretion. So there will be both a growth in bureaucracy and in bureaucratic discretion. This is allied to the view that like everyone else, people in the public sector are self-interested and will seek to maximise their own interests which are allied to the size, status, and scope and salaries of bureaucracies. If this development is linked to the scope for discretion then you have a recipe for a great increase in bureaucratic power which, because a lot of it is discretionary, will not be accountable. It will be dominated by producer interests.

- A further criticism of the social justice approach is that it creates dependency and does not recognise reciprocity and obligation. That is to say, if people come to depend on the state as a fundamental way in which they can satisfy their needs, they will become passive, dependent, detached from the labour market etc. Also there will grow up a culture of entitlement which does not recognise any link between a right to resources and a duty to discharge a range of obligations.

This will lead to a decline in civic virtue.

Possible responses

There are, of course, ways of responding to all of this. First of all, the argument about liberty/ability. This is defective for various reasons.

- Freedom and ability cannot be as categorically distinct as the classical or economic liberal argues because:
  - any attempt to explain why we value liberty must be linked to an idea of ability. We value liberty because with it we are able to do things which we can't do without it. That is to say, the value of liberty is justified in terms of ability. Given this, liberty must involve a concern with the resources and opportunities which impact upon ability;
  - a generalised ability to do something is a necessary condition of determining whether a particular individual is free or unfree to do it. Before the invention of aeroplanes, and thus a generalised ability to fly, it did not make sense to ask whether an individual was free or unfree to fly. Hence freedom and ability are logically linked;
  - if liberty is entirely negative, that is to say, to do only with the absence of coercion, then the question of whether one society is more or less free than another is a matter of counting up the number of coercive rules in each society. This is surely wrong. If you asked, in 1980, whether Britain is a freer country than Albania, surely a count of the rules in the society would not yield a reasonable answer. Given that Albania was pretty primitive with very little traffic and virtually no financial system, it may well be that it had fewer rules prohibiting conduct than the UK. But what made the UK a freer society is what we were able to do then which people in Albania were not, for example, criticise the government/emigrate etc. Again liberty and ability are closely linked. While of course negative liberty in terms of freedom from interference is important, positive freedom – the freedom/ability to do things and having the appropriate resources and opportunities – is also vital and was central to both the Social Liberal and Social Democratic traditions.
- We cannot bypass the question of whether market outcomes are just/unjust by arguing that the issue does not arise because these outcomes are unintended. The reason for this is that intention is only a part of the issue at stake. In ordinary life we are held responsible not only for the intended consequences of actions but also for the foreseeable (although unintended) consequences. So, even if market

outcomes are unintended, they are broadly foreseeable: those with the fewest resources, the least human capital, living in communities with the lowest degree of social capital will enter the market with least and as a group, leave it with least. This is not intended, but it is entirely foreseeable. We can therefore be said to bear some collective responsibility for this and that the situation is unjust. It is the role of the state to correct, as far as possible, remediable injustices and therefore the state has a clearly defined moral role here.

- Economic liberals put a great deal of weight on Hayek's argument about moral pluralism and the difficulty about arriving at agreed criteria of distributive justice. This can be overplayed. First of all, the question is one about a degree of consensus rather than truth. That is to say, we are looking for broadly accepted criteria of distribution within a particular society at a particular time and not for some kind of perfect moral objectivity which may well be unobtainable. This is an issue that can only be addressed by democratic deliberation (economic liberals are very suspicious about democracy) so that through democratic means some kind of broad consensus can be reached about what government should be doing to rectify injustice.

- This brings us to the point about interest group competition which the economic liberal believes will occur in the absence of agreement about social justice. There is something in this argument, I think, and a government embarking on a project to create greater social justice needs to create a degree of consensus about the principles underlying its approach, because ultimately this will be the only way of facing down coalitions of interest groups engaged in rent seeking behaviour. Gordon Brown has written an interesting chapter in *Crosland and New Labour* (Leonard, 1999) about this problem.

- There is also something in the economic liberals' critique of bureaucracy both in terms of size and performance/discretion. There are, however, ways of tackling this within a Social Democratic state rather than claiming that because the problem of bureaucracy exists, the Social Democratic project should be abandoned. Agency status, cash limits, citizens' charters, league tables, regulation, state funding rather than direct state provision, contracts and the funding for the voluntary sector (which Beveridge was very keen on), are all ways in which the producer interest aspects of the public sector can be tamed so as not to highjack the social justice project.

- Dependence/obligation. There is nothing in Social Liberal/Social Democratic approaches which would sanction a neglect of these things. The ideal of the Social Liberal and the Social Democrat has been an active and inclusive citizenry, and if social policies have indeed created dependence and a lack of recognition of obligation and civic virtue, then there are plenty of moral resources in each of these movements for seeking to challenge such policies. Central to the Social Democratic ideal has been the notion of autonomy. If there is good empirical evidence that a particular form of welfare creates dependency, then this will underline the role of personal liberty, dignity and autonomy.

Social justice today

I want to use this point to move to the positive argument for social justice which, from my perspective on the government, would be something like this: social justice is the central value of the Social Democratic/Social Liberal tradition. In our present circumstances we need to accept that with the growth of the role of the market and all the changes to markets that are a consequence of globalisation, then social justice and welfare are going to have to go with the grain of the market. We have to recognise that the situation of those with few skills and low human capital situated in communities with low social capital are suffering and will continue to suffer from social injustice unless we agree to take collective responsibility for the situation. Expecting such people to become active in the labour market would be like compelling people to play football without being concerned whether they have football boots. So a project about social justice has to recognise this collective responsibility and invest in the skills necessary to equip people to make their way in a market-based economy. At the heart of the project will be work and the labour market since, whether we like it or not, work in our society is the main vehicle through which individuals and families gain a sense of dignity, worth, self-respect, a stake in society and escape from poverty. Putting investment in the skills for the labour market at the centre of social justice fits with the idea of positive freedom – of increasing people's ability. It will also secure a good degree of electoral consensus because of the central role that work plays in having a sense of worth in society. It is also important in the context of Beveridge and a lecture in Toynbee Hall to emphasise the improvement in social capital as well as human capital if we are to achieve greater social justice.

Today we talk in terms of social capital. The older generation like Toynbee and others talked about civic idealism rather than social entrepreneurship, but they are alike in seeing a central collective responsibility here.

But there are two issues which I would have thought that a speech on social justice in the Beveridge context should address.

- We should not expect a work-oriented approach to social justice to be cheap. There will be large input costs improving human and social capital and there is a massive job to do in this respect. Equally there will almost certainly be very large and continuing output costs. If the private labour market does not produce enough jobs particularly for low-skilled people (which there will still be, however hard we work on employability skills), and if we are making work a basic obligation of citizenship, then we have to be prepared to provide the means by which this public/civic obligation is to be discharged. This will be on either continuing public subsidies to private sector employers, public money for non-skilled jobs in the public sector or money for jobs in the voluntary sector. That is to say, a work/skills-oriented approach to social justice will not come cheap and it is difficult to see how we shall arrive at some kind of plateau of expenditure. Nevertheless, it is the right and the first thing to do, but as an exercise in social justice it will have to be underpinned by a degree of consensus about the moral imperative here to support the public expenditure necessary.

- What about social justice and those who cannot work, or are past the end of their working life? Beveridge was clearly in favour of the insurance principle for both unemployment benefits and for pensions. The government has a much more mixed economy of welfare view here and certainly is pushing for more tax-funded/means-tested benefits. The problem as Beveridge saw it and as it was seen subsequently is that those on means-tested benefits (National Assistance in Beveridge's day) were seen to be stigmatised and second-class citizens. What are the principles informing the government's view of the role of social justice for those inevitably outside the labour market? Are benefits for those who have not/cannot benefit from insurance-based entitlements going to be set at a level to guarantee a decent level of social inclusion if not a greater degree of social/economic equality for those on benefits? I do think the government has to go beyond 'work for those who can, security for those who cannot' because security can mean anything across a spectrum, from a minimum safety net to being linked to some kind of greater equality measure such as average wages. The problem of moving to the greater equality end of the spectrum, of course, is that work incentives are decreased. Nevertheless, I believe that if we are to talk about social justice and social inclusion we need to talk about those people outside of the labour market as well as those within it. The government has secured a great degree of support for its social investment approach to social justice via its link to work but it does need to address those not in the labour market. It would be odd, as I have said, to find a lecture on these themes at a Beveridge event without discussing this group.

Equality, social justice and poverty

Broadly speaking there are three approaches to the understanding of poverty: relative poverty, absolute poverty and what might be called the 'moving absolute' view. On the relative poverty view, of course poverty and inequality are linked because poverty is defined in terms of a consumption or income norm, for example, the European Union's position of being below half the average wages. It becomes inevitable, therefore, that anti-poverty programmes on this view are linked to policies to diminish inequality. The second approach which is not now widely accepted is the absolute view, where the poverty line is fixed at the level of income below which it is not possible to satisfy subsistence needs or a basic calorific intake. On such a view of poverty, though, there is no link between poverty and inequality. Public spending and the welfare state are there to provide a minimum to prevent destitution *not* as under the previous approach to act as an instrument to improve the relative position of the worst-off.

The final view was one adopted by the Thatcher government in effect. It rejected the relative view of poverty and saw the conceptual problems in trying to define a minimum. What the new view proposed was that the success of policy should be seen in terms of whether the lowest decile in society are better off in their own terms this year than they were last year. That is to say, we do not worry about a growing gap between rich and poor: rather, what matters to the poor is not the gap between them and some other group but whether they are better off in real terms on a year-by-year basis. Indeed, on this view, greater inequality may be necessary to ensure that this year-by-year improvement takes place in that the best chance of improving the position of the poor is a dynamic market economy which will create a 'trickle-down effect' to improve the position of the poor in the ways that I have suggested.

Quite different political strategies are implied by these different views of poverty.

Social Democrats have tended to adopt the relative view of poverty and the strategy becomes: use public expenditure (financed by the fiscal dividends of growth) to improve the relative position of the worst-off while maintaining the absolute position of the better-off.

Economic Liberals accept the absolute approach and their strategy is the reverse of the Social Democrats: improve the absolute position of the worst-off on a year-by-year basis and accept that the relative position of the better-off will improve as the result of the incentive consequences of the market economy.

This is a pretty basic political divide and one issue for the government to resolve is whether talking the language of social inclusion will lead them to the economic liberal direction: that is to say, we improve the employability skills and the social capital of the worst-off and over time their incomes will rise *but* not necessarily in such a way as to diminish inequality. Or is it that the tax implications in the long term of policies of social inclusion will mean eventually that inequality will diminish because the tax implications imply a degree of redistribution from the better-off to the worst-off?

Note

[1] Many historians would consider Beveridge to be a 'Progressive' rather than a 'New' Liberal. See Harris (1997) and Clarke (1974).

References

Clarke, P. (1974) 'The progressive movement in England', *Transactions of the Royal Historical Society*, vol 24, pp 159-81.

Harris, J. (1997) *William Beveridge: A biography*, 2nd edn, Oxford: Clarendon Press.

Green, T.H. (1888) 'Liberal legislation and freedom of contract', in R. Nettleship (ed) *Works of Thomas Hill Green, vol III, Miscellanies and memoir*, London: Longmans, Green and Co, pp 365-86.

Joseph, K. and Sumption, J. (1979) *Equality*, London: John Murray.

Leonard, D. (ed) (1999) *Crosland and New Labour*, London: Macmillan.

EIGHT

Conceptions of social justice

Julian Le Grand

In thinking about social justice, it is important not to use ideas that violate people's intuitions as to what is fair or just. It is both foolish and impolitic to try to impose some top-down principle of justice that would lead to situations being described as fair that most people think are manifestly unfair, or consider situations to be unjust that most would consider just. What is needed is a conception of justice that is firmly rooted in people's intuitions; one that is general enough to command consensus, but specific enough to yield useful policy prescriptions.

One such conception relates social justice to the extent that individuals have control over their own lives. It states that, if one individual is deprived relative to another *due to social factors beyond their control*, then that situation is unjust.

The roots of this conception derive from the fact that our attitude towards the justice of individuals' position in life is affected by any knowledge we may have of how they got into that position. We cannot simply observe two people with different incomes and then decide that this situation is unjust; we need to know the factors that have contributed to their poverty or wealth, and whether they have control over those factors. For instance, suppose we discover that the two had equal ability, but one of them lived in a deprived area with poor schools while the other grew up in a wealthy district with good local schools. The individual from the wealthier area got the A-level grades to go to university and went on to a professional career, while the equally-able individual from the poor area, because of inadequate schooling, had to take an unskilled job on a low wage. In those circumstances, most people would consider the resultant inequality in their incomes to be unjust – because it was caused by factors beyond their control. But compare this situation with two similar individuals, again both of equal ability but this time both with access to an equally good education. One on leaving college chose a demanding, but high-paying job, whereas the other preferred a quiet life and chose to go into less stressful, low-paid employment. In that case, the inequality in their incomes would not be regarded by most people as unjust – even though that inequality may be the same or even greater than in the first case – because it arose from the free choices of the individuals concerned.

So the more control that people have over their lives, and the fewer are the social barriers that restrict their overall life chances, the more likely the society is to be just. This idea is a simple one, but one often unrecognised by many advocates of income redistribution. Taking income from the rich and giving it to the poor will cause resentment – because it will be regarded as unjust – if it does not acknowledge a difference in the routes by which people become rich or poor. If someone is wealthy because, starting from a lowly background, they worked hard to overcome the social barriers they face, then their situation is quite different from one whose riches arise from an accident of birth or geography. Similarly, if someone is poor because, although heir to a fortune, they have frittered away their wealth and opportunities, then their claim for compensation is different from that made by someone without their advantages. (They might have a claim on our *compassion*, but that is not the same as a claim based on justice; as the proverb says, 'be just before you are generous'.)

Moreover, simple redistribution may be socially inefficient as well as socially unjust. If those who work hard or those who save find their income redistributed away, then this will have an impact on their incentives to work and save. If those whose position is the result of their own efforts or actions are treated in the same way as those whose situation is a result of social factors beyond their control, then the impact on both social justice and social efficiency – through the effect on incentives – could be very damaging.

It should be noted that the emphasis in this conception of justice is on the 'social' factors that are beyond individual control. There are, of course, many 'natural' factors that affect people's life chances but that are also beyond their control: genetic inheritance being the most obvious. But it does not seem to be thought unfair that some people are born with better looks, more strength, greater ability, etc than others. Nor is it regarded as unjust if such people earn greater rewards because of those factors: even the huge incomes of rock stars or footballers arising from their native talents do not seem to generate social resentment. Hence, inequalities arising from these kinds of factors seem to be rather different from inequalities arising from social differences – another illustration of the point that policies aimed at promoting social justice cannot be based simply on the fact of inequality, but have to take account of the *route* by which people get their wealth.

Another reason for emphasising the 'social' over the 'natural' is that, almost by definition, social factors are the ones that society can do something about. For social factors are barriers to opportunity and inclusion created by the society; and what society has created, it can knock down. There is not a great deal that the government can do about the fact that some people are born with good looks or a strong physique while others are not. But poor schooling, bad health facilities, race and sex discrimination – all of these are social factors that reduce some people's opportunities compared with others, and all are amenable to government action.

As this suggests, this conception of social justice has powerful implications for policy. It implies that we cannot achieve justice by relying on redistribution through taxes and benefits alone. For that could be, as we have seen, both unjust and inefficient. What are needed are policies aimed at equalising people's life chances: policies that give people, especially those from socially excluded families or communities, more control over their lives; policies that give them greater choice and opportunity. Education is obviously a key to this; so is health. Unskilled people do not have the opportunities open to them that skilled ones do; the unhealthy cannot fulfil their potential in the way that the healthy can. Inequalities in education and in health are perhaps the biggest sources of injustice in our society today; reduce these (as the government has committed itself to do) and we will have a much fairer society.

This is not to say that there is no place for redistributive tax and benefit policies. The dictates of both social justice and compassion will require the provision of cash benefits and services for those whose natural disadvantages are such that no education or health system, however fairly distributed, can compensate. Social compassion will also require the provision of a safety net to catch those who fall because they make mistakes or are reckless or improvident. It might also be necessary to tax the rich (even the 'deserving' rich) so as to reduce the extent to which they can buy privilege for their children (although it is worth noting that the impact of at least one of the ways in which they do this, private education, can be ameliorated by achieving higher standards in state schools).

So Beveridge-style welfare benefits still have their place. But the emphasis needs to shift. It is no longer sufficient to rely on benefits and taxation to achieve social justice. Rather we need to concentrate on policies that are designed to give everyone a greater equality of life chances; for that is the way to achieve a society that is not only efficient and modern, but also socially just.

NINE

Equality of access

Peter Kellner

Beveridge, 57 years on

As the Prime Minister has often remarked, British society is vastly different from the 1940s:

- people live longer (therefore have longer in retirement);
- health technology and costs have soared;
- more single parents, broken marriages;
- no longer the case that almost all fathers worked, while almost all mothers stayed at home with their children;
- more private consumption, and ownership of goods (and houses, cars, electrical appliances etc);
- more people face deep-seated, long-term unemployment problems;
- less faith today in government to provide perfect, all-knowing solutions (the war was probably the high point, historically, of faith in central government – after all, it was the government, not the market, that organised victory over Hitler).

The fundamental objectives of welfare policy have not changed – to slay the 'five giants' identified by Beveridge – but different strategies are now needed.

Three key (and linked) propositions:

- People should take whatever responsibility they can for their own lives.
- Responsibility can be exercised effectively only within a healthy social and economic framework.
- The role of government is:
  - ‣ to maximise the capacity of people to take responsibility for themselves;
  - ‣ to help create and support a healthy economic and social environment;

▸ to ensure that provision exists to help people surmount obstacles they cannot tackle on their own.

(Note: 'to ensure that provision exists' means just that – it does not necessarily mean organising provision directly. Compulsory motor insurance is an example where the law lays down what people must do, but the government then leaves a regulated market to deliver the insurance.)

It could be argued that these principles underpinned Beveridge's own thinking – and that his report offered a 'special case' solution related to the circumstances of his time.

If there is a unifying idea it is that of *mutual responsibility*. I expanded on this in my pamphlet, *The new mutualism* (1998). In this context, 'mutualism' is not about cooperatives or building societies, but about the basic relationships between citizens, communities, employers and the state.

I summarised my argument in 'the seven pillars of mutualism'; these could help to underpin a new 'Beveridge Mark Two' philosophy of welfare, community and government action.

1　For a free society to flourish, the exercise of individual liberty requires the acknowledgement of mutual responsibility.
2　Mutualism can thrive only when it is rooted in culture and choice, rather than laws and coercion; it should be encouraged as far as possible, and enforced only when necessary.
3　Legitimate economic and political power may derive from a variety of sources; what matters is how it is used, how it is checked and how far it is dispersed.
4　Markets are social institutions that should both offer rights to, and demand obligations from, those who seek financial gain.
5　Government has a duty to promote responsible market behaviour; to act as an effective umpire it should, as far as possible, avoid being a market competitor.
6　Mutualism requires an inclusive society in which all have equal access to the means to participate in it to the full.
7　Government has a duty to guarantee basic equality of access, but should, as far as possible, leave delivery to independent institutions exercising their mutual responsibility.

Equality of access

I won't repeat my detailed thinking here. (It's all in my pamphlet.) I would, however, draw attention to 'equality of access' (points 6 and 7); this could provide a more fruitful way to pursue equality than 'equality of outcome' or 'equality of opportunity'.

Here is a brief version of my argument.

'Equality of access' is underpinned by three principles:

- whatever form equality takes, the principle should apply to everyone at all times: to rich and poor, to men and women, to black and white, to those who pass exams and those who fail them;
- when the principle of equality is invoked, it should be for its own sake, not merely as a stepping stone to some wider social objective;
- equality is ultimately about humanity, not money. In practice money often matters hugely, but it is a means to an end, not the end itself. And there are some forms of inequality that money cannot cure.

Equality of access casts its net far wider than equality of outcome and equality of opportunity. It is concerned not just with the skills and material means that contented citizens need, but with information, power, security, health and justice. It is about rights at work and the freedom to walk through the streets without fear. 'Equality of access' proposes that a mature democracy should strive for a range of equal membership rights for all its citizens, involving parity of access to those things that, together, comprise a just and healthy society. Here is a provisional list:

Everyone should have equality of access to …

- the ballot box;
- the information that enables people to hold to account those who wield power, public and private, in their lives;
- competent, affordable representation when in discussion or dispute with those who wield power;
- safe and peaceful neighbourhoods;
- fair treatment by the police and courts;
- reasonable, affordable housing;
- healthy, affordable food;
- prompt and appropriate medical treatment when needed;
- (for children and young adults) education that will enable people to achieve their full potential as adults;
- (for adults) employment that does not violate the employee's dignity or health.

That list doubtless contains defects and omissions. However, it seeks to set out a range of issues in which (in the view of this writer, at least) equality has an intrinsic virtue. The most obvious example is the ballot box: every elector should have one vote. Equality of the franchise is the essence of democracy. Even here, though, the emphasis is on access rather than outcome. An elector may choose to abstain. Elections are decided by those who vote, not by those who stay away. The key thing is that every elector should have equal *access* to the ballot box.

Or consider food. Too many inner-city households, especially single-parent families, live in 'food deserts'. Supermarkets and good greengrocers are beyond easy reach to those without cars; local corner stores charge high prices and sell little that is fresh and in good condition. For people living in food deserts, equality of access is partly about income and partly about the nature of our retail system. Some means of coaxing Tesco and Sainsbury's to set up small 'metro' supermarkets in poor housing estates might help as much as an increase in social security benefits to achieve equality of access to healthy, affordable food.

The argument here is that poverty is not the only problem, nor higher state benefits the only answer. Some poor people have easy access to supermarkets; some less-poor people do not. If an information under-class does develop, it will include some less-poor people (especially older men and women who are terrified by computers); many younger people will know their way around the information superhighway, even if they have little money. True equality of access takes account of such points; equality of outcome does not.

Likewise – indeed, even more so – with healthcare. Most people depend on the National Health Service. Its quality affects almost every family. Does it provide everyone who needs it with prompt and appropriate treatment? Or are there groups who have worse access than others – the inarticulate, elderly people, residents of the wrong region or the wrong part of town? More subtly, does the (probably inevitable) concentration of the most modern, high technology facilities into fewer, larger hospitals, give car owners an advantage over less mobile citizens?

'Equality of access' goes further than 'equality of opportunity' and is more realistic than 'equality of outcome'. At the same time, it avoids ideological rigidity. It does not demand a particular form of economic organisation, or ownership of industry, or tax regime; it does not prescribe a particular maximum range of incomes; nor does it say that wealth is bad. Rather, it invites those, inside and outside government, who design policies for the economy and social security, industry and education, the police and the health service, transport and housing, to measure the impact of their plans against equality of access criteria.

Equality of access sets challenges not only to policy makers but to the operation of market forces. Nothing proposed here challenges the basic principles of flexible and efficient capital and labour markets, or the use of incentives. What is proposed is that the consequences of market forces need to be monitored: if and where they violate the objective of equality of access, then action should be taken to rectify matters. Solving the problem of 'food deserts' or improving bus services to large hospitals are examples of where market forces need a firm nudge.

Equality of access also provides a fresh framework for tackling social exclusion. That the poor need more money; that their plight has got worse over the past 20 years; that welfare benefits are often inadequate; all these things are beyond doubt.

The issue is not the description we provide of a dysfunctional society, but the vision we offer of a healthy one. The argument here is that equality of access could provide a large part of that vision. One reason is that equality of access is multi-dimensional, concerned not just with money but with the full range of matters that determine whether people can enjoy the full fruits of citizenship.

References

Kellner, P. (1998) *The new mutualism*, London: Co-operative Party.

TEN

The balance of rights and responsibilities within welfare reform

Alan Deacon

This note discusses how rights and responsibilities may be balanced in the context of the three themes which have been central to New Labour's approach to date.

The idea of a 'Third Way' which encompasses and reconciles policies and approaches previously regarded as antagonistic (Blair, 1998). In the case of welfare this involves a recognition that there is a need for *both* a broader redistribution of income *and* for policies which are focused upon and demand more of the long-term poor. The work of Robert Walker, John Hills and others on 'the dynamics of poverty' has fundamentally changed our understanding of the nature of poverty and deprivation. Their analysis of longitudinal data has demonstrated that it is not a problem of poverty but of different forms of poverties which have different causes and require different policies. In particular they have identified the trajectories through which people move in and out of poverty and the events and personal characteristics which make them more likely to experience poverty (Hills, 1998; Walker and Park, 1998). Tackling these will require a greater honesty and candour about the role of behaviour in social pathology than was shown in academic and political debates for much of the post-war years. At the same time it is important to heed Philip Selznick's warning of the dangers of a 'selective concern' with 'personal virtues, personal morality' and consequent neglect of communal responsibilities. As he emphasises, "personal responsibility is most likely to flourish when there is genuine opportunity to participate in communal life. These conditions require substantial investment by the community and its institutions" (Selznick, 1998, p 62)[1].

The idea of social exclusion as a dynamic process. The recognition that poverty is not a static condition and that the poor are not homogeneous does not in itself resolve arguments over causation. It would be only something of a caricature to distinguish between an 'Old Labour' view of the poor as excluded by external structures and processes and a New Right view of the poor as excluded by their behaviour and culture. Effective policies cannot be based upon either of these simple models. Nor can they be based upon 'a bit of each'. What is required is more in the nature of a compound than a simple mixture, which reflects the complexity of individual decision making. There are few who respond directly to economic incentives in the way which economists often suppose, and fewer still who are mired in a culture of dependency. Moreover, there is now a considerable literature which documents how people respond as creative moral agents to issues of partnering and parenting, and are well able to balance competing needs and obligations (for example, Smart and Neale, 1997; Williams et al, 1999). In policy terms there is no simple combination of compulsion, financial sanctions and rewards, and moral suasion which fits all circumstances.

The idea of an enlightened self-interest which provides both a basis for a renewal of popular support for welfare and a rationale for the use of compulsion to prevent people excluding themselves from society (Deacon, 1998). Appeals to the enlightened self-interest of the electorate emphasise that a fairer, more cohesive society can be expected to experience less crime or incivility. Such appeals are all the stronger, however, if it can be demonstrated that the recipients of welfare are fulfilling their reciprocal obligations, or are being required to do so. Nevertheless, it is the second sense in which the term is used which is most relevant here: the use of welfare to encourage, cajole, or compel people to act in ways which are unattractive to them in the short term but can be expected to reduce the risk of them becoming socially excluded in the longer term.

These three themes can be illustrated briefly in respect of two issues which are currently at the forefront of the welfare debate: the extension of the New Deal to lone parents and the introduction of stakeholder pensions.

The New Deal for lone parents

This issue illustrates better than any other the conundrum that underpins much of the welfare debate. Public policy needs to formulate rules which can be applied fairly and consistently across individuals and groups of individuals. Yet it is ever harder to map such frameworks onto a growing diversity of work arrangements and care obligations. The growth of part-time, temporary and 'flexible' employment – primarily undertaken by women – has eroded the distinction between paid work and non-work. This in turn has rendered redundant the long-standing debate as to whether lone parents are to be categorised and provided for as workers or as carers.

The lowering of the threshold for Family Credit to 16 hours a week reflected these changes and created the potential for a greater flexibility of provision for those already doing some paid work. The key issue, however, is those who are currently outside the formal labour force. A lone parent in the UK is not required to register for work until his/her youngest child is 16. It is almost universally accepted that this is a major reason why the proportion of lone mothers in paid work is now lower than it was in 1971, and is little more than half the proportion of married mothers in work. In consequence the proportion of lone mothers dependent upon Income Support has almost doubled since 1971, with self-evident implications both for government spending and the numbers of lone parents in poverty (Miller, 1998). There could hardly be a clearer example of benefit rules which enable – even encourage – claimants to exclude themselves from the labour market and thereby restrict their opportunities for wider participation (for a recent discussion of this issue, see Lister, 1999).

There is, therefore, an overwhelming case for requiring the majority of lone parents to accept a greater responsibility to seek work and/or enhance their employment skills. As a first step they should be required to participate in the 'New Deal' when the youngest child is 13. This age should then be lowered subsequently to 11, and then eventually reduced to eight. There is, of course, a case for lowering the age still further. That would be at the least premature given the ambivalence of popular attitudes to the role of lone mothers and the very real uncertainties about the quality of the childcare available to them (Morgan, 1998; Phillips, 1997). In the meantime those not required to participate in the 'New Deal' should remain subject to the regulations made under the new Welfare Reform Bill regarding attendance at an initial interview.

It would be important to recognise caring responsibilities, and so the lone parent of a disabled child should be exempt from this requirement, as should any lone parent in the first year after bereavement or separation.

Those lone parents who are required to participate in the New Deal should benefit from the same employer subsidies as other participants. Another possibility would be to pay a significant premium to Child Benefits/Income Support rates in respect of children under six, but to pay more for older children within Family Credit and the new Working Families Tax Credit. It has to be recognised that such an enhanced role for Family Credit/Working Families Tax Credit is open to the criticism that it is simply replacing one form of benefit dependency with another, since wages will be a small proportion of the total income of someone working for only 16 hours a week. It also has to be recognised that there is discouraging evidence that the rules for Family Credit have in the past served to discourage claimants from working longer hours or seeking better paid jobs (Green, 1998). In the medium term, however, it is hard to see any alternative to accepting this danger as the lesser of two evils and seeking to minimise it through amendment of the regulations.

The introduction of 'stakeholder' and 'second' pensions

Pensions reform faces the same difficulties of attempting to map clear and uniform rules onto a diversity of work and family patterns. The recent Green Paper rests upon the principle that those who are able to make provision for their retirement should do so, but that the government should secure a decent income in retirement for those who are not able to provide for themselves.

The decent income is to take the form of a means-tested Minimum Income Guarantee (MIG). The Green Paper recognises that, as a means-tested benefit, MIG will penalise voluntary savings among the current cohort of pensioners (DSS, 1998). This is unavoidable in the short term, given the prohibitive cost of a universal guarantee. What is important, however, is that the level of the guarantee should rise with age to a greater extent than is currently proposed[2]. This is justified both by the greater needs of older pensioners and by their lack of opportunities to make their own provision in the past[3]. It would have to be mirrored in the new second pension, if this is to provide a margin over MIG at all ages (see below).

No government is going to commit itself to a specific definition of a decent minimum. A reasonable target, however, would be a guarantee that a couple of age 75–84 should receive the equivalent of the minimum wage for one person for a full working week (Jupp, 1998)[4].

The key issue in respect of those able to make provision for their pension is the extent to which they should be encouraged or compelled to accept their responsibilities. The Green Paper reflects the view that compulsion should be limited to ensuring that people do not unnecessarily become a burden on others, that is, everyone should provide themselves with at least the equivalent of the MIG. It is difficult to fault this as a principle. To compel people to do more would be an unwarranted restriction of autonomy. To do less would be to allow people to exclude themselves.

There are, however, two points which follow from this. The first is that the level of the compulsory second pension must provide a substantial margin over the MIG and avoid the need for other means-tested benefits such as Housing Benefits or Council Tax benefits. Thrift must be rewarded, even when it is involuntary. The second point is that the 'encouragement' to take out a stakeholder pension must be real not token. The government will find itself in an absurd position if it is saying to (for example) a worker in his/her twenties, 'You must take out a stakeholder pension, we will give you financial inducements to do so. But if you ignore our exhortations and disregard our incentives, we will still ensure that you will have a decent income in retirement'. The implication of this is that the government should state now that the level of the MIG will be progressively reduced from (say) 2030[5]. Government promises to pay higher pensions in the future have not always been kept, but a commitment to reduce them will presumably carry greater conviction.

Beveridge's solution – social insurance

Beveridge was fully aware of the ways in which welfare impacted upon the attitudes and behaviour of claimants, and his Report was clear that assistance should not be provided in a manner which condoned any breach of 'citizen obligations'. Indeed, he noted in his first private memorandum to the officials who advised him that any scheme left those "assisted unnameable to economic rewards or punishments while treating them as free citizens is inconsistent with the principles of a free community"[6].

Beveridge's solution was, of course, to enable people to meet their responsibilities through National Insurance. The scheme he proposed is now inappropriate since it envisaged that entitlement would be based upon contributions paid by those in work. Modern social insurance – such as that put forward by the Borrie Commission – needs to extend eligibility to those who are not economically active, particularly carers.

It is social insurance which best embodies the idea of a contract between government and citizens. It is highly unfortunate, therefore, that the government has set its face against the principle of social insurance. There are several aspects of the new Welfare Reform Bill which will further erode the coverage and value of insurance benefits. It proposes, for example, to reduce Incapacity Benefits paid to those with an occupational pension. The essential point, of course, is that Incapacity Benefit is paid to compensate for the extra costs of disability. To reduce it for occupational pensioners is to punish and penalise those disabled people who have sought to act responsibly and make provision for themselves.

Notes

[1] Equally apposite is David Ellwood's warning that the danger with "dynamic research is its tendency to look to the individual as the critical behavioural unit". This means that it lends itself more easily to "questions such as 'what is wrong with those people?' than to questions such as 'what is wrong with that society or economy?'" (Ellwood, 1998, p 57).

[2] The rates of MIG proposed in *Partnership in pensions* increase by roughly 3% for persons between 75-84 and by a further 5% for persons over 85. As a first step the differentials should be widened to 5% and 10% respectively.

[3] Older pensioners are more likely to be single, more likely to be women, less likely to have any part-time earnings, more likely to be frail, more likely to have higher living costs – for example, arising from restricted opportunities to use lower-cost supermarkets – and more likely to have exhausted their savings or other capital.

[4] The degree of age-relation proposed here would mean that a pensioner couple 65-74 would receive 95% of this rate, a couple aged 85+ would receive 110%.

[5] The impact upon an individual pensioner would, of course, be offset in part by the age-relation of MIG.

[6] The ways in which Beveridge sought to minimise the impact of welfare upon the behaviour and character of those who received it is discussed in Deacon (1996).

References

Blair, T. (1998) *The Third Way. New politics for the new century*, London: Fabian Society.

Deacon, A. (1996) 'The dilemmas of welfare', in S. Green and R. Whiting (eds) *The shifting boundaries of the state in modern Britain*, Cambridge: Cambridge University Press, pp 1-11.

Deacon, A. (1998) 'The Green Paper on welfare reform: a case for enlightened self interest?', *Political Quarterly*, vol 69, no 3, pp 306-11.

DSS (Department of Social Security) (1998) *Partnership in pensions*, Cm 4179, London: The Stationery Office.

Ellwood, D. (1998) 'Dynamic policy making', in L. Leisering and R. Walker (eds) *The dynamics of modern society*, Bristol: The Policy Press, pp 49-62.

Green, D. (1998) *Benefit dependency*, London: Institute of Economic Affairs.

Hills, J. (1998) *Income and wealth: The latest evidence*, York: Joseph Rowntree Foundation.

Jupp, B. (1998) *Reasonable force. The place of compulsion in securing adequate pensions*, London: Demos.

Lister, R. (1999) 'Reforming welfare around the work ethic', *Policy & Politics*, vol 27, no 2, pp 233-46.

Miller, J. (1998) 'Family obligations and social policy: attitudes, behaviour and policy change', 14th Congress of Sociology, July, Montreal.

Morgan, P. (1998) *Farewell to the family?*, London: Institute of Economic Affairs.

Phillips, M. (1997) *The sex-change state*, London: Social Market Foundation.

Selznick, P. (1998) 'Social justice: a communitarian perspective', in A. Etzioni (ed) *The essential communitarian reader*, London: Rowman and Littlefield, pp 61-71.

Smart, C. and Neale, B. (1997) 'Good enough morality? Divorce and post-modernity', *Critical Social Policy*, vol 17, no 4, pp 3-27.

Walker, R. and Park, J. (1998) 'Unpicking poverty', in C. Oppenheim (ed) *An inclusive society. Strategies for tackling poverty*, London: Institute for Public Policy Research, pp 29-52.

Williams, F., Popay, J. and Oakley, A. (1999) 'Changing paradigms of welfare', in F. Williams, J. Popay and A. Oakley (eds) *Welfare research: A critical review*, London: Taylor and Francis, pp 2-16.

C Social justice into practice

ELEVEN

The New Right and New Labour

David Piachaud

The New Right and New Labour's inheritance

After 18 years of Conservative government there was:

- more poverty – one third of children living in families under half average income level;
- more inequality between rich and poor;
- more dependence on state benefits, particularly means-tested benefits;
- more homelessness and people living on the streets.

The changes had been driven by the philosophy of the New Right, seeking to roll back the state and rely on markets with only residual social welfare. This philosophy had powerful attractions. As Keynes wrote:

> **The Economists were teaching that wealth, commerce and machinery were the children of free competition.... But the Darwinians could go one better than that – free competition had built Man. The human eye was no longer the demonstration of (God's) Design, miraculously contriving all things for the best; it was the supreme achievement of Chance, operating under conditions of free competition and laissez-faire. The principle of the Survival of the Fittest could be regarded as a vast generalisation of Ricardian economics. Socialistic interferences became, in the light of this grander synthesis, not merely inexpedient, but impious, as calculated to retard the onward movement of the mighty process by which we ourselves had risen like Aphrodite out of the primeval slime of Ocean. (Keynes, 1927, pp 13-14)**

Yet as Keynes' essay on the end of laissez-faire continued:

> **This is what the economists are *supposed* to have said. No such doctrine is really to be found in the writings of the greatest authorities ... the popularity of the doctrine must be laid at the door of the political philosophers of the day, whom it happened to suit, rather than the political economists. (Keynes, 1927, pp 17-18)**

The New Right's espousal of individualism, and laissez-faire has been a failure. Social spending went up, not down. Numbers on social security went up, not down. Universal education and healthcare remain.

The New Right has lacked any effective ideas in response to social ills such as drug addiction, racial discrimination or environmental problems. Law and order cannot be left to the free market. The New Right's assumption that private market provision was necessarily good was seen to be as dogmatic as the Old Left's presumption that it was necessarily bad.

Shortly before she was dumped by her own party, Mrs Thatcher said: "I hang on until I believe there are people who can take the banner forward with the same commitment, belief, vision, strength and singleness of purpose". Clearly John Major failed this test. Now that he has discovered 'compassion', William Hague is in danger of failing too. But compassion is not an add-on extra, a sticking plaster to hold together the crumbling carcass of Conservative thinking. There can be no genuine compassion without social justice. The New Right and the Conservative Party remain monumentally indifferent to social injustice. The New Labour government is committed to tackling it.

New Labour's start in tackling social injustice

New Labour's strategy has four main distinguishing features:

- **Tackling the causes of social injustice:** In the past social welfare policies have been unduly concerned with casualties, with picking up the pieces, and with doing things *for* people. Much more attention in social policy is devoted to dealing with social problems than to preventing problems. More attention is focused on outcomes than on opportunities. Yet welfare handouts are no substitute for independence and the opportunity to produce for oneself. Opportunities depend on employment opportunities, on education, on training, on rehabilitation, on housing. Most people are only too keen to stand on their own feet. But this is difficult without a secure foundation.

- **Emphasising responsibilities as well as rights:** In the past most of the emphasis has been on individual rights. Yet all of us have mutual responsibilities. Unemployed young people have a responsibility to train or take work. Absent parents have financial responsibilities towards their children. Government, too, has responsibilities. Emphasising these responsibilities does not abolish rights; it makes them sustainable.
- **Focusing help on those who need it most:** Beveridge in his Report assumed there would be a universal national health service and allowances for all children. These do and will remain. But, where appropriate, focusing available resources on those who need them the most is one means of tackling social injustice.
- **Promoting all forms of welfare:** Beveridge's Report was concerned with *Social insurance and allied services*, what is now often called social welfare. In the 1950s Richard Titmuss wrote that welfare, like Gaul, could be divided into three parts: *social* welfare produced through social services, *occupational* welfare produced through employment, and *fiscal* welfare produced by means of the tax system. Much research on caring suggests that Titmuss' threefold division needs extending to a fivefold division: to the other three forms must be added *voluntary* welfare, produced by unpaid work in the community, and *family* welfare, produced by immediate family members. This last is responsible for the greatest part of social care; sharing of income within the family is responsible for the greatest component of social security. All these forms of welfare are important.

This broad strategy is designed to promote work for those who can, security for those who cannot.

This strategy is being put into practice in employment with economic policies. To promote growth, the Welfare to Work programme and childcare initiatives. Inequality in earnings and net incomes are being tackled through the minimum wage and the Working Families Tax Credit. In education improved basic standards are being promoted and truancy tackled. Social exclusion is being addressed, for example, through the proposals for the worst estates in *Bringing Britain together* and through support for carers.

All these measure are all about promoting opportunities and empowerment and tackling the causes of injustice.

Challenges and choices

The New Labour government has made a start.

The challenge of promoting social justice is as great as it is worthwhile. It cannot be claimed that everything has been done right.

The task of the welfare reform roadshow was to explain why welfare needed reform. Looking back it is now perhaps clearer that most people agreed there was a need for reform. The challenging issue is not *whether* but *how* to reform welfare.

Taking one step at a time, without presenting each step as part of a broader strategy, undermined confidence. For example, what was done on One-Parent Benefit can now be seen in a broader context in relation to extensions of childcare and the new Working Families Tax Credit.

Focusing on promoting 'work for those who can' may obscure the fact that the government is firmly committed to security and a share in rising prosperity for those who cannot work. As the Green Paper on welfare reform stated:

> **We are acutely aware of the fears that even talk of welfare reform can arouse. For some, benefits are their lifeline. So we must approach reform sensitively and with the full engagement of the whole country. (DSS, 1998, p iv)**

A second requirement – perhaps a challenge for some – in the struggle against social injustice is not to pretend we now have all the answers. Past policies were clearly inadequate; poverty rose despite rising social security expenditure. Present policies represent a substantial and significant start. But there is much more to learn and to do.

Lessons must be learned from abroad.

In many respects other European countries are more effective in promoting social solidarity and confidence in social welfare and in tackling social exclusion than Britain.

In the USA the 1996 Welfare Reform Bill has led to the removal of large numbers from welfare rolls. But as the former Secretary of State for Labour, Robert Reich, wrote:

> **We have no way of knowing how many of these people are in permanent jobs paying a living wage, or are in temporary jobs paying so little that they have to double up with other family members and leave their children at home alone during**

the day, or are living on the street. (R. Leich in *Times Literary Supplement*, 22 January 1999, p 4)

Drawing lessons from the USA on welfare reform has been likened to taking a course from David Beckham on stress management.

The government must be prepared to experiment, monitor the results and learn. This has long been the practice in the health service. Government must be humble enough to do it for other social policies – and strong enough because not every experiment will be successful.

The government must be, and is, prepared to be judged by what is done and what it achieves. Last month Alistair Darling announced an annual audit setting out how the government is confronting and tackling the causes of poverty.

Politics is about priorities and trade-offs. The burden and consequences of political choice are not removed or lessened by presenting issues as though there is no choice or freedom of manoeuvre. It must be acknowledged and accepted that there are many difficult choices to be made:

- Empowerment involves responsibilities and rights. We must recognise that if personal responsibilities are extended then implied rights dependent on the state become more important. For example, to be successful the Welfare to Work programme depends on full employment opportunities.
- There is no clear and unchanging boundary between public and private spheres. For example, steps to increase the protection of children against abuse within their own family have inevitably increased government intervention in the previously private world of the family. Defining this boundary between public and private is fraught with difficulties, yet government has responsibilities which requires it to do so. Not everyone will ever agree, as controversy over the Child Support Agency attests.
- Helping people into work will help many low-income families. For example, the new Child Care Credit will help many mothers. But many mothers, and a few fathers, in low-income families choose to remain at home when their children are very young. How far should priority be given to the employed parents over those not employed – but still working very hard?
- Extending opportunities and encouraging people to help themselves requires a secure foundation. Beveridge recognised this very clearly. Focusing help on those in greatest need through means testing can

reduce incentives to work and save. A balance must be found but the dilemma is inescapable.

- While it is important to tackle area-based problems – for example, through the Social Exclusion Unit's pilot projects – it is important to recognise that most of the poor are not in pockets of poverty. Even the best-off areas, the City of Westminster for example, contain many who are poor.
- While Welfare to Work and the Single Gateway help thousands into work, we must recognise that the major determinant of youth and long-term unemployment is the overall level of unemployment. The state of the economy is therefore crucial to poverty and social justice.

The centrality of social justice

The New Labour government has made a start, but only a start. It must continue its pursuit of social justice. Common humanity demands it. As Aneurin Bevan wrote in his book, *In place of fear*:

> **"After the first death, there is no other." With that lovely and tender line the poet Dylan Thomas ends a poem on the death of a child killed in a fire-raid on London. The poet here asserts the uniqueness of the individual personality. If the imagination can plumb the depths of personal tragedy, no multiplication of similar incidents can add to the revelation. Numbers can increase the social consequences of disaster, but the frontiers of understanding are reached when our spirit fully identifies itself with the awful loneliness and finality of personal grief. (Bevan, 1961, p 199)**

The capacity for emotional concern for individual life is the most significant quality of a civilised human being. It is not achieved when limited to people of a certain colour, race, religion, nation or class. Indeed, just to the extent that this group or that group commands our exclusive sympathy, we are capable of the most monstrous cruelty, or at best indifference, to others who do not belong to the group.

Apart from common humanity, any democratic government must justify its legitimacy. This in turn depends on the underlying rules being accepted as fair. Democracy cannot thrive without social justice.

Contrary to what some people suggest, there is not a choice between wealth creation and redistribution. Certainly without the wealth there can be no redistribution. But without the redistribution that spreads education and opportunities to all there would be far less wealth creation. Nor is it only the private sector that creates wealth. An NHS hospital creates as much or more wealth as a private hospital. Voluntary organisations, such as many of you work for, create wealth. The family in nurturing, educating and civilising children creates wealth.

Better ways of creating wealth need to be found that cascade down to the poorest, the most excluded, the marginalised. That is a formidable challenge. If all the poorest get is a meagre trickle, the crumbs from the rich man's table, that is not enough – it is not acceptable.

The government has said it cannot go back to the 'tax and spend' policies of Old Labour. Not all agree, but the fact has to be faced that in the past greatly increased social spending simply did not succeed in reducing social inequality. On the other hand, it is possible to make public spending more effective in promoting social justice. And it is possible, without increasing tax rates, to make tax a more effective instrument for social justice by curbing tax evasion and clamping down on schemes whose only purpose is to deprive the Exchequer of the resources needed to promote social justice.

Nor is it only British poverty and inequality that should be of concern to the government. A third of the world's children go to bed each day hungry; every day 30,000 children die from preventable diseases. Over one billion people live in the direst poverty. Some of the poorest countries are crippled by accumulated debt. The British government has endorsed the goal of halving the population in absolute poverty by 2015. It took the lead with the G7 finance ministers in speeding up the writing off of debt. Much more remains to be done.

In the world there is growing interdependence both within nations and between nations. For an integrated cohesive and civilised world, there must be opportunities for all children everywhere. No society can long flourish in which a minority – whether determined by income, class, gender, colour or creed – is socially excluded and devoid of power. Equally a peaceful world is ultimately dependent on a just distribution of wealth and power.

As Beveridge realised, the notion that our society or the world can advance through the pursuit of individual self-interest alone is not only false, it is also dangerous. The pursuit of social justice is at the core of the government's purpose. It has made a start.

References

Bevan, A. (1961) *In place of fear*, London: MacGibbon and Kee.

DSS (Department of Social Security) (1998) *New ambitions for our country: A new contract for welfare*, Cm 3805, London: The Stationery Office.

Keynes, J. (1927) *End of laissez-faire*, London: Hogarts.

TWELVE

A modern party of social justice: achievements and missed opportunities

Ruth Lister

This note assesses the government's record in promoting social justice under the four, sometimes overlapping, headings of:

- tackling social exclusion and poverty;
- supporting and investing in families;
- 'a new contract for welfare';
- strengthening and extending citizenship.

Each section is divided into achievements and missed opportunities, although in some cases the same policy represents both an achievement and a missed opportunity.

Tackling social exclusion and poverty

Achievements

- The establishment of the Social Exclusion Unit at 'the heart of government' in the first few months in power. The Unit's reports display a seriousness of purpose in tackling the problems within its remit. The strategy for neighbourhood renewal is particularly impressive and has generally been well received.
- The proposed annual poverty audit. This should act as an important marker of the government's commitment to reduce poverty and provide a focus for public debate on anti-poverty strategies.
- Recognition of the need to address the link between poverty and health inequalities.

Missed opportunities

- The opportunity now exists to build on these initiatives to promote a high profile, comprehensive anti-poverty strategy which is more than the sum of its parts, in line with the Declaration of the 1995 Copenhagen Summit on Social Development. In particular such a strategy needs to be:
  - *Participatory:* The speed with which the Social Exclusion Unit has had to work has made it difficult for it to engage in genuine consultation with those affected by the problems it is tackling. As acknowledged in the neighbourhood renewal report, policies to tackle social exclusion are unlikely to work if the communities affected are not involved in their development. There is an opportunity now for the Social Exclusion Unit to translate this principle to the national level and, in collaboration with voluntary agencies such as the UK Coalition against Poverty, to design a participatory infrastructure. This would provide channels through which those excluded from the formal political process could participate in debates about policies to tackle social exclusion and poverty, as was the case in the development of the Irish National Anti-Poverty Strategy. The process of engagement which this would entail would strengthen the fabric of citizenship.
  - *Comprehensive:* The focus on discrete problems and groups in the Social Exclusion Unit's remit, while perhaps necessary initially to ensure quick results, runs the risk of encouraging the belief that these groups are themselves 'the problem' and of obscuring the underlying processes and structures which lead to social exclusion in its various manifestations. It also underplays the importance of low incomes. Again, there is an opportunity now to apply the principle of 'joined-up thinking' to an analysis of how government can tackle these underlying causes, which are not confined to lack of a job.
  - *Focused on a target:* The proposed annual poverty audit would be given more bite if linked to an explicit poverty reduction target, as agreed in Copenhagen. This would complement the government's goal for reducing world poverty.

Supporting and investing in families

Achievements

- The 1998 and 1999 Budgets both represented an important acknowledgement of the need for improved financial support for families with children. The increase in Child Benefit and the extra help to families on Income Support were particularly welcome.
- The childcare strategy is a breakthrough in its recognition that childcare is a public as well as a private responsibility. With adequate resourcing, it should mean that the UK no longer lags way behind fellow members of the European Union.
- The adoption of the parental leave directive likewise represents recognition of public responsibility for helping parents combine paid work and family responsibilities, in line with EU thinking.
- The Sure Start initiative demonstrates the importance of cross-departmental thinking in addressing the need for more support for and investment in families with young children.
- While any assessment of whether the proposed reforms of the Child Support Act have 'got it right' would be premature and foolhardy, the acceptance of the case for a disregard for those on Income Support will mean that children on Income Support will, at last, see immediate gains from the Child Support Agency.
- The national strategy for carers provides important recognition of the value of the work undertaken by carers, even if not adequately resourced, and a partial corrective to the government's heavy emphasis on paid work as 'the' expression of citizenship responsibility.

Missed opportunities

- There is a danger of piecemeal policy making in relation to financial support for children. There is now an urgent need for a more comprehensive review of financial support for children based on the available evidence about the needs of children of different ages and in different kinds of families. The indication in this year's Budget of the long-term goal of a 'single seamless' income-related payment for children, built on Child Benefit, provides a unique opportunity for such a review. The result should be to strengthen policy making in relation to both families and poverty.
- The impact of the parental leave directive will be limited so long as

the leave is unpaid. A longer-term strategy to build on the immediate implementation would also provide the opportunity to address a central issue raised in the recent Millennium Lecture (on the work and leisure balance, given by Jonathan Gershuny at No 10 Downing Street, 27 January 1999). In order to encourage male involvement in the care of children, some Scandinavian countries now reserve a month of the parental leave for fathers, with some success.

• The 'carer's package' would be strengthened by improvements in the invalid care allowance. It is paid at a lower level than contributory benefits and its status as an independent benefit is compromised by the fact that entitlement is tied to receipt of other benefits by the person receiving care.

'A new contract for welfare'

Achievements

• The New Deal schemes represent a major investment in tackling the poverty and social exclusion associated with worklessness. Paid work *is*, for many (though not all) people, the best route out of poverty.

• Minimum wage and tax-benefit policies 'to make work pay' should help to tackle poverty among those in work, even if criticisms can be made of aspects of their implementation (including the likely transfer of resources from many mothers to fathers as a result of the Working Families Tax Credit).

• The principle of 'security for those who cannot work' is helpful and reminds us of the need to put the 'security' back into social security. (Whether all of the policies which are emerging will provide that security is more debatable.)

Missed opportunities

• The comprehensive review of welfare represents a number of missed opportunities:

  ‣ It is the latest in a series of reviews which have failed to address the central question of the adequacy of benefits to meet human needs. The opportunity to develop a 'minimum income standard' against which benefit levels can be judged, as called for by the

European Commission, has not yet been taken. Such a standard could represent an important symbol of the government's commitment to social justice.

- The welfare reform process has side-stepped the crucial issue of the balance between contributory, means-tested and categorical (subject to neither contribution nor means-tests) benefits. There is a danger that incremental decisions on individual benefits will shift that balance significantly without proper public debate. Moreover, the future of social insurance, the linchpin of the Beveridge Plan, remains unclear. Social insurance reflects the spirit of a welfare contract and of the interrelationship between rights and responsibilities which informs the reform strategy. Yet, the opportunity to revitalise and modernise social insurance, as recommended by the Commission on Social Justice, has not been taken. The end result is likely to be a further move down the poverty relief model of social security which has proved less successful than more comprehensive models in combating social exclusion and poverty.

- Despite the emphasis on modernisation in the face of social change, the welfare reform process has so far not addressed two key trends identified in the Green Paper on welfare reform:

    i) the changing position of women and the inappropriateness of a social security system still largely predicated on male employment patterns (in particular the assumption that people work either full time or not at all) and a male breadwinner model. This also raises the difficult issue of how caring responsibilities can best be recognised in the social security system which is only beginning to be addressed;

    ii) the "rise of the demanding, sceptical, citizen-consumer" (DSS, 1998, p 16). No attempt has yet been made to apply to social security the principles of 'user-involvement' developed elsewhere in the welfare system.

- There appear to be no plans to reform one of the most contentious elements of the 1986 Social Security Act: the social fund. Although it represents only a fraction of the overall social security budget, the social fund has a particular significance as the safety net beneath the safety net. The evidence from research and the voluntary sector is that it is failing in its objective of focusing help on those in need.

- The emphasis on paid work in social security policy opens up the opportunity for the better integration of social and economic policy which has not been fully grasped. If the policy of 'reforming welfare around the work ethic' is to be successful in the long term, greater priority needs to be given to reducing worklessness in economic policy and more needs to be done to build ladders up out of the marginal jobs most likely to be available to workless people.

Strengthening and extending citizenship

Achievements

- Constitutional changes such as the implementation of the Human Rights Act, which serve to strengthen citizenship, are also part of the social justice agenda. The government has made great strides on this front. Of particular significance is the Northern Ireland Peace Agreement and its promise of 'just and equal treatment for the identity, ethos and aspirations of both communities' – a statement which recognises that social justice involves both equal treatment and respect for difference and diversity.
- Similar principles underpin the progress which is being made in strengthening the civil rights of disabled people and the position of women through the establishment of a Women's Unit in the Cabinet Office.
- Devolution, together with initiatives such as the People's Panel, the Race Relations Forum and Listening to Women, help to promote active citizen involvement in governance.

Missed opportunities

- The review of the treatment of asylum-seekers provided the opportunity to demonstrate the government's commitment to internationalism and to "an outward looking Europe, not a fortress against outsiders" (Blair, 1998, p 18). The removal of all right to benefit from this group has sent out the very opposite message.
- Overall, more could be done to improve the position and influence of minority ethnic groups in the creation of "a diverse but inclusive society" (Blair, 1998, p 12), especially in the wake of the Stephen Lawrence Inquiry. More generally, the commitment to a new, more inclusive politics and to listening to the people points to the need

directly to strengthen the 'voice' and citizenship of members of excluded groups and users of the benefits system, as suggested above.

- The recent recognition of the value of care work and of other unpaid forms of work (cf speech given by the Prime Minister at the Annual Conference of the National Council of Voluntary Organisations, 21 January 1999), in contrast to the emphasis on paid work in social security policy, could open up a much-needed debate about the relationship between paid and unpaid forms of work and the value we accord to each. (For example, participation in unpaid voluntary/ community work could be incorporated into the welfare contract, as it was in the Australian Working Nation programme.)

- The sheer scale of support for the government at and since the General Election provides a unique opportunity to create a constituency of support for building a more just society. More could be done to capitalise on this. Instead, there is a danger that the negative language used about benefits and benefit claimants could be counterproductive and divisive. And welcome as measures of 'quiet redistribution' have been, the positive case needs to be made for (fair) taxation as an expression of our responsibility to one another as citizens, in order to build long-term support for such measures.

References

Blair, T. (1998) *The Third Way: New politics for the new century*, London: Fabian Society.

DSS (Department of Social Security) (1998) *New ambitions for our country: A new contract for welfare*, cm 3805, London: The Staionery Office.

THIRTEEN

Social security: a cornerstone of modern social justice

Robert Walker

The argument

Social security – defined to include social assistance (America's 'welfare') – is the great facilitator: it enables economic and social progress to be achieved, demographic and individual change to occur.

It protects the incomes and rights of individuals who suffer the consequences of the economic and social change that benefits the community as a whole. By minimising personal distress, it prevents the social unrest that might otherwise inhibit economic and social advance.

Social security provides individuals with the time and resources to adjust to new circumstances, to rebuild their lives after personal catastrophe and misfortune. It enables them to plan and to save for the future, to create personal security and financial independence.

Social security binds society together through a system of mutual obligation and sharing. By ensuring that the extremes of poverty and wealth are avoided, it fosters the personal independence and interdependence that underpins democracy. By risk–pooling and sharing, society confers individual security.

Britain led the world with the post-war Beveridge reforms: comprehensive social security (National Insurance), universal social assistance (National Assistance). Society's safety net remains very effective by international standards, although social insurance benefits are comparatively low (Eardley, 1996). Britain is still a world leader in the provision of occupational and second tier pensions and in integrated Welfare to Work programmes.

Social security is not just a mechanism, it is a goal for society and each of its citizens. Social security helps to define and underpin individual well-being and social justice.

Social security is weakened when the sense of shared interest is lost or loosened. This happens when social security is restricted to the few and used by a minority. Focusing on the cost of social security in isolation from either its purpose or achievements can have the same socially disintegrative effect.

Rejection of the system can result in the rejection of those who are intended to be its immediate beneficiaries. Claimants, who are despised, may come to despise themselves – and to reject those who first despised them.

Most benefit recipients who are castigated for being passive and dependent on the state are unfairly criticised. Almost all claimants of working age have aspirations of independence but lack the wherewithal to achieve them (Shaw, 1996; Trickey et al, 1998). Pensioners are justly receiving the rewards for their past contributions as workers and taxpayers; very few have willingly squandered their wealth to live at society's expense.

Social security is more solution than problem. It is justice in action. Political expediency caused previous governments to deny this reality. Voters may have done likewise, eroding popular support for what, in reality, is a bulwark of both modern justice and the perpetuation of democracy (Stafford, 1998).

Rebuilding faith in social justice requires the reinstatement of social security in a central, positive role. Social security, based on mutual obligation and accountability between citizens and their government, is a key to modernising Britain and a reason for doing so.

Advances in social justice

The following are good examples of social security reforms that have fostered and sometimes redefined social justice.

Development of social assistance, 1943 and 1966

Nationally uniform scale rates, based on regulation rather than discretion, promote social and national cohesion, and enhance territorial justice (that is, they avoid entitlement being dependent on place of residence).

The principle of universalism, with benefits made available to all people solely on the basis of need, reduces discrimination and stigma and limits the risk of people falling into destitution. It also enhances flexibility and adaptability: the system automatically copes with new social risks without the need for primary legislation.

Family Allowances and Child Benefit, 1946 and 1979

These benefits foster cohesion by sharing the cost of social reproduction, reduce life-course inequality in income, and lessen the risk of childhood poverty. They also promote work incentives.

Unification of Housing Benefit in 1972/73

As a response to Beveridge's failure to take adequate account of geographical variations in housing costs, local authorities introduced a myriad of different rent subsidy schemes. In 1972/73 these were unified and, although further reform is now required, unified Housing Benefit enhanced equity of treatment and provided tenants with protection in a hostile housing market.

Development of non-contributory disability and carers benefits, 1975

These reforms created rights for disabled people who had never been able to acquire a contribution record and recognised the additional costs of disability that can lower living standards and foster social exclusion. They also provided public recognition of the social contribution made by carers although women carers were subjected to discrimination until 1987.

Introduction of Family Income Supplement, Family Credit and Working Families Tax Credit, 1972, 1988 and 1999

Britain was one of the first countries to offer financial assistance to low-income families in work, creating social solidarity across the employment divide, rewarding effort and enhancing work incentives. The *national minimum wage* furthers these objectives and seeks to ensure that work is adequately rewarded.

Creation of executive agencies, committed to enhancing customer service, 1990s

Extending rights to good service provision in the public sector is both socially inclusive and life-enhancing; it challenges the destructive maxim that 'the poor get poor service'. Unfortunately, the opportunities presented by these reforms were never fully exploited (Walker et al, 1995). New Deal and related policies present a second chance.

New Deal, 1998

Building on Jobseekers' Allowance, New Deal policies offer advice, support and services in addition to income. They are designed to assist people to attain greater self-sufficiency while enforcing the obligations inherent in welfare receipt. Social security is accompanied by social support. It is important, however, that paid work is never presented as the only route to citizenship, since this would lead to a loss of dignity and exclusion among those for whom work is not an option.

Proposed pension reforms, 1998

Government proposals will enhance social justice for pensioners. The development of stakeholder pensioners and providing credits to carers will reduce income inequalities among retired people, as will pension splitting on divorce.

Counter examples

There are also, though, many examples of decisions that have undermined popular faith in the legitimacy and effectiveness of social security, eroded its power to unite and made it seem to be an instrument of injustice.

Subsistence-level social security, 1948

The original decision not to pay insurance-based benefits at a significantly higher level than means-tested ones prevented the development of a strong commitment to social insurance among wide sections of the populace, and reinforced the perception of social security as a refuge for society's failures. Social security in Britain has always been about the relief of poverty, rather than about community and justice. This has lessened the cohesive influence of social security and the electoral support it has enjoyed. Europe offers a number of alternative models.

Lack of partnership, 1940s onwards

There has been no role for communities, trade unions, social entrepreneurs or industry – except as the providers of competing services

– in the design and implementation of social security. Social security has been the government's problem to resolve, rather than society's creation to be nurtured.

De-indexation, 1980

The link between pension levels and wage inflation had virtually eradicated extreme poverty among elderly people by the late 1980s. Abolishing the link not only resulted in considerable individual hardship, it also created resentment among many older people (Bradshaw and Lynes, 1995). This has, in turn, engendered distrust among younger people in the ability of society to deliver on the social contract between generations (Stafford, 1998).

The abolition of State earnings-related pension scheme (SERPS), 1988 and 1995

The curtailment of SERPS further reduced the public's faith in the trustworthiness of government and its ability to deliver universal security in old age. It undermined the contract inherent in social insurance and encouraged underprovision of pension coverage among the groups most at risk of experiencing poverty in old age.

Targeting housing subsidies, 1980s

The shift away from bricks and mortar subsidies created substantial financial barriers to work for social tenants. This, accompanied by the indiscriminate sale of council housing and the failure to promote and properly manage social housing, led to social polarisation and to pockets of worklessness.

Concealing unemployment, 1970s and 1980s

The use of disability benefits and early retirement to reduce the unemployment count encouraged benefit recipients to leave the labour market prematurely. This may well have undermined the autonomy and self-respect of many of those affected. It may also have blurred the distinction between unemployment and incapacity benefits in the eyes of the public, eroding the 'legitimacy' of welfare, and encouraging later generations of unemployed benefit recipients to adopt a similar strategy.

Policy vacuum on youth unemployment, 1980s and 1990s

The failure in the 1970s and 1980s to respond adequately to the collapse of job opportunities for poorly qualified school leavers, the provision of on-the-cheap training and work experience and removal of social security benefits created an underqualified and perhaps disaffected cohort of young people. It may also have caused subsequent generations to undervalue education, training and self-reliance.

Labour market policies, 1980s and 1990s

The failure to contain the growing wage inequalities exacerbated the financial disincentives of benefit provision, and necessitated benefit systems that serve as wage subsidies. Likewise, the failure to engineer a smooth transition into work that sensitively reflects the availability of casual and part-time work, may unnecessarily trap some people in prolonged worklessness and encourage others to join the informal economy.

'Spinning' social security as a problem, late 1980s and 1990s

Much harm was done by targeting social security for cuts, justifying these by overstating the unsustainability of expenditure and necessarily reneging on social contracts in the process. This was exacerbated by coining 'welfare dependency' as a pejorative term and by replaying the social myths of scroungers, fraud and abuse. These eroded popular support for social security and exacerbated the stigma and social exclusion experienced by bona fide claimants who constitute the vast majority of welfare recipients.

Social Fund, 1988

This reform successfully capped expenditure on the exceptional and one-off needs of benefit recipients by replacing a rights-based system by discretionary cash-limited loans and grants. This created a lottery for beggars, a lasting scar on Britain's social security system (Huby and Dix, 1992).

Opportunities

There are enormous opportunities to use social security to extend social justice and to strengthen the social contract upon which it is built.

Positive social security

Social security should be promoted for what it is: an essential, supportive element in the drive to modernise Britain and to rebuild a commitment to social justice. Obligations on welfare recipients should be accompanied by citizen rights to adequate benefits and a testable government commitment to quality service.

Social Europe

Social security is an essential element in the process of economic integration in Europe, minimising the individual hardship that might result in pursuit of the common good. As social security supported the creation of nationhood in the 19th and 20th centuries, reforms in the 21st century will foster the development of a Social Europe.

Service delivery and citizenship

Prioritising effective service delivery can enhance the self-esteem and social integration of benefit recipients. Moreover, the contract inherent in social security is two-way, as should be the accountability. A proven commitment to work for those who can should be matched by a public commitment to provide a quality service that is responsive to the needs and aspirations of users. Excellent access, information, advice, support and responsiveness help people to help themselves. Social security is the 'people's bank'; the concept of social or community banking provides a useful model for future development.

Social security 'plus'

New Deal marks the end of passive social security. But for the most hard to help, financial and employment assistance is only the start. Poor housing, ill-health, family problems, learning difficulties, substance abuse, are typically part of the complex equation that causes social exclusion. Single Gateway should provide access to comprehensive information, advice, advocacy and service provision to address these other impediments to self-sufficiency.

Ending the 'low pay, no pay' cycle

The challenge, after the success of New Deal, is to help sustain people in work and to tackle the 'low pay, no pay' cycle in which larger numbers of people are trapped. This means post-benefit support to encourage job retention and progression, and the opening of existing training and advisory opportunities to recipients of in-work benefits and other people in insecure employment. Accompanying 'welfare to work' by 'welfare in work' would foster employment security and financial self-sufficiency while reducing flows of claimants onto benefit.

A community service

Rightly national in design and coverage, social security is nevertheless delivered locally. It could be, perhaps should be, a community service. User consultation, local management boards – as in France – or, even, local franchises for service delivery could improve services and foster collective support for social security. But local responsibility would need to be matched by adequate resources and support to ensure continuity and quality.

A national Housing Benefit

Even in the absence of much needed fundamental reform of Housing Benefit and housing finance, there is still a need radically to improve the administration of the benefit. The quality of service provided by local authorities is highly variable and acts as an impediment to Welfare to Work and benefit security. Relaunching Housing Benefit as a national service, operated by local government or other local franchisers according to user-orientated service agreements, could improve the lives and security of millions of people, both old and young.

Integrating generations

New Deal is an important first step in breaking the spiral of disillusion arising from the failure of training and employment schemes to deliver transferable skills and qualifications valued by employers. But the young face injustices and anomalies created by the benefit system (especially

Housing Benefit), while older workers confront age discrimination in employment and potentially a harsher benefit regime. Addressing these issues would decrease disaffection and withdrawal from the labour force and the legitimate economy into non-citizen status ('Status Zero').

References

Bradshaw, J. and Lynes, T. (1995) *Benefit uprating policy and living standards*, Social Policy Reports No 1, York: Social Policy Research Unit, University of York.

Eardley, T. (1996) *Social assistance in OECD countries*, Synthesis Report, DSS Research Report 46, London: HMSO.

Huby, M. and Dix, G. (1992) *Evaluating the Social Fund*, Department Research Report, London: HMSO.

Shaw, A. (1996) *Moving off Income Support: Barriers and bridges*, DSS Research Report 53, London: HMSO.

Stafford, B. (1998) *National Insurance and the contributory principle*, In-house Report No 39, London: DSS.

Trickey, H. et al (1998) *Unemployment and jobseeking: Two years on*, DSS Research Report 87, London: HMSO.

Walker, R., Brittain, R. and Brittain, K. (1995) *Benefits agency customers and the 1994 review of the benefits system*, In-house Report No 7, Leeds: DSS.

FOURTEEN

Making welfare work[1]

Polly Toynbee

The need for a new consensus

There is a search party out for some big new idea, an overarching vision that will define and rationalise the whole untidy social security system. Welfare reform was promised at the election, and all heads nodded wisely. The idea that we spend far too much, and don't spend it well, has been strongly promoted by the Prime Minister himself. Reform can sometimes sound rather more like a threat than a promise.

Although Britain spends less than most other Western nations on social security, although a life on Income Support is undoubtedly one of abject poverty, although we have had a Conservative government for 18 years committed to rooting out fraud and scrounging, the fact remains that there is very little public trust in the integrity and efficiency of the benefit system. Nor is there an obvious guiding principle to encourage support for it and, alas, all too few political advocates over the years willing to promote it. Political capital has all been invested in promising to squeeze, cut or even throttle it. But trust and support for social security urgently needs to be restored, because the real value of benefits will otherwise continue to diminish with the poor getting even poorer, which is not only wicked in itself, but immeasurably damaging to the fabric of society for everyone else. We need to reach a stage where there is broad public support for a strategy of increasing benefits.

For millions of poor people money may not be the only, or even the single most important thing that can improve their quality of life, but money is a sine qua non.

Most people can agree on what the social security system is there to do. It is to give those who genuinely cannot earn their living a decent life roughly comparable with the rest of us – though exactly how much so will always be in dispute. Social security is there to help the truly helpless while weeding out the idlers. However, most people would also agree that the system is Byzantine and incomprehensible. Recent research shows how little its own users understand it. It is an odd fact that even people who count themselves generally well informed about most other aspects of government look blank and alarmed if asked to explain something as basic as, say, Family Credit. Wait until we get to the Working Families Tax Credit and see who understands it!

The government's promise of reform has led many people to think that there is some kind of simple sense to be made out of social security. While I think the intentions and principles of social security can be greatly clarified, giving it back a renewed credibility and social purpose, much of its complexity is, alas, inherent and unavoidable. At its simplest it can be described as a security blanket ensuring no one ever freezes to death, but that blanket is actually a patchwork quilt of great intricacy made up of very different patterns, paid for and paid out in quite different ways for different reasons. Each separate square has a history, an ideology, an intention of its own. It is stitched together with many ideas, not with one.

The myth of social insurance

Beveridge's great trick was to pretend that there was a single grand design. The words National Insurance covered a multitude of different elements, very few of which actually did what people thought. They thought it paid for the whole NHS when it pays for only a token fraction. They thought there was a fund they had paid into to have a right for life to draw out of, when in fact it was always up to the whim of government to vary the value of benefits. Above all, Beveridge's fundamental fraud was his failure to find politically acceptable ways to raise entitlements for sickness, unemployment or old age to reach the National Assistance, or now Income Support level, that would ensure that no one who had paid in would ever have to be means tested. It never was proper insurance, because from the very beginning, anyone without any other income had to be topped up, so it made scant difference to them whether they had paid their contributions or not. Two poor pensioners standing in line at the Post Office always drew out the same sum, even if one had paid stamps for years and the other had never paid a penny. In other words, National Insurance was always something of a con – a big idea, but a muddled reality. Its great advantage was to pretend to bind together the rich and the poor, to persuade the better-off to fund a system that paid out largely to the worse off.

The idea of giving everyone rights sounded good even if those rights were useless, as most people were still means tested. Then, as now, it would be too expensive and wasteful, to pay out non-means-tested entitlements at a rate that would cover a reasonable standard of living both to those who do, and those who don't, need it. Older people, and some younger ideologues, still talk today of the wonders of the National Insurance idea, and it has a very nostalgic ring these days. Most people under, say, 40, who remember nothing of its origins, have only the haziest notions of what those National Insurance deductions from their pay packets are, and on what principle they differ from Income Tax. Most people have no idea what they might be entitled to in sickness or unemployment, until they find themselves having to claim it. Ask other people to differentiate between National Insurance benefits and other benefits, and how their entitlement arises, and they do not have a clue.

The end of universalism

The ideological link has been all but lost between the big idea and the patchwork of benefits on offer. I would go so far as to suggest that many current National Insurance and universal benefits have exactly the opposite effect on the well-off than that intended by Beveridge. Those with high incomes are bemused to be offered Child Benefit, unemployment and sickness pay and maybe even pensions, when they plainly don't need them. It doesn't necessarily make them feel good about the system. It does not give any serious incentive to make them more willing to participate in redistribution. Their views on that would be largely ideological, and unlikely to be driven by insignificant sums they might get back now and then. On the contrary, for many, receiving automatic payouts only confirms the inner suspicion that the social security system is lax, extravagant and feckless. It is paying out to people like them who don't need it; how much easier to believe all those 'Shock! Horror!' tabloid stories about vast, idle families drawing huge weekly sums.

I have often used myself as an example and I know I am a rare case, but I was astonished to receive over £120 per week widowed mother's benefit, on the death of my husband, without anyone asking whether I needed the money or not. I know it is counter-intuitive but my hunch is that affluence testing of benefits for the best-off would increase their trust in the system in the long run. They would still pay in. It would still be insurance, but people could only draw out if they ever fell into real hardship.

So the time has come to redefine what we mean by National Insurance. It should no longer be an arbitrary payer out of benefits to people on the grounds of some life events, like illness, losing a job or even old age. We should redefine it as the guarantee against poverty, a much easier and more coherent idea to grasp. Of course it has to be done slowly with advance warning, and especially with pensions, phased in over a great many years. If, say, one third of people will never benefit from pensions because they fall below the Income Support threshold, one third who get the payments, don't really need them because their income is getting higher with each newly retiring cohort, then we have a great edifice in place designed only to reach the one third in the middle. Nor is it entirely clear why they should get more than those in the one third below them. This redefinition of what we mean by National Insurance wouldn't save huge sums, but it would make quite a lot of money available to target on the most needy. I believe that redirecting those funds would be largely acceptable and comprehensible to the losers.

However, saving money is not the primary intention. It would send out the message that all social security money paid out is well targeted on genuine need. It would shore up trust and support for the system. Taken from those according to ability to pay, paid out to those only on the grounds of need, clarity and integrity would be restored to what has become a very weird shaped and ragged social security blanket.

A new emphasis on work

That is one simplification and clarification. So far the government has propounded its own big idea for the social security system – Welfare to Work – and it is an excellent one. It has a clear resonance that rings like a bell. Beveridge always said that "benefits were only supposed to be paid to those who, without doubt, couldn't work". Since his time, hard years of unemployment have blurred the lines, and there is a strong popular belief that many are drawing benefits who could find work. True or not, it has undermined faith in the social security system that needs to be restored. However, quite apart from its good public relations, there is little doubt that Welfare to Work is likely to be a great social good in its own right, because whatever people say about 'Mac-Jobs', almost any job is better than none for workless households.

Take the evidence on single mothers. The children of those with jobs do as well as those children of married couples, while the children of those mothers without work fall behind in achievement. Even a routine job is status among people profoundly alienated, lonely and lacking in any sense of belonging to the rest of the world. Giving them every encouragement, extra money and a bit of a push is the right thing to do for the sake of those people's own happiness. To be sure, we have to start building ladders up from the first lowly jobs, to turn them into a reasonable prospect of a career with training and the hope of betterment. All the same, the jump up from no job to first job is a great life change for many.

However, Welfare to Work serves another important purpose – underpinning trust in the social security system as nothing else can. If all the talk, activity, interest and innovation in social security centres on the project of getting people into work, it will reassure cynics about the integrity of all benefits. It sends out the message that all who can are working even if low incomes are topped up with extra benefits, even if there are few or no overall savings. If it is seen to work well, it follows that those who are still on Income Support will be well understood to be in genuine need, deserving of sympathy and a reasonable standard of living.

In his second Budget, the Chancellor started what is to be hoped will be a continuing trend towards increasing Income Support levels. He has already laid the foundation for giving differential increases to pensioners, giving more to those on Income Support than the rest – something that should be built on even if it grieves those who do have small savings and don't gain as much. Through the ideas of Welfare to Work we have a framework heading in the right direction, which should allow for a steady growth in Income Support levels. Of course the tapers will always be difficult: wherever the taper ends there will be some who are aggrieved, but it is often the complaint of the non-prodigal son who rightly gets rather short shrift in the parable. Those with small savings, small pensions or earning just above wherever Family Credit or Income Support eligibility is set, will have to put up with the rising prosperity of those just beneath them.

The exception of Child Benefit

The other key change in direction in the second budget was the increase in Child Benefit. Despite what I have already said about the need to abolish automatic entitlement to benefits, Child Benefit is the one exception. It is a different piece of the patchwork altogether from the National Insurance entitlements, with a different purpose and very different effects. It is the best bridge between welfare and work, helping to remove work disincentives. Given the huge increase in the proportion of children who are born into poverty it is a well-targeted benefit too and one to be built on. The Chancellor has already said that he will tax it in future, and I see no reason why he shouldn't claw the whole of it back from top-rate taxpayers or their partners. My guess is that there would be relatively little dissent as long as all the money saved is paid towards giving more to the poorest families. But the key principle of paying it in the first place to every mother must remain, even in those families where the whole lot is taken back, in order to retain its present full take-up and to keep the wallet to handbag effect. This is still surprisingly important in quite affluent families where mothers don't work.

So, now it is time to stop talking about social security as if it were the measure of failure in any society. It is time to persuade people to take more pride in it as a symbol of success. They should be proud when we no longer have homeless beggars on the street, or old people too poor to turn on their heating, or children with so much less than their peers that they are stigmatised from their first day at school. But that requires political leaders to feel some pride in it themselves. It is not an unfortunate excrescence or murky backwater. Decent benefits wisely distributed are the best badge of a nation's social identity and moral intentions. By the end of this government let's hope the cheers will be raised in speeches not by how many cuts have been made in any minister's nasty little list, but by how much people's lives have improved – some through work, all through a better standard of living. Welfare will be working when all work who can, all who can't are well provided for, and all society feels proud of both achievements, trusting the system well enough to be willing to pay for it. I don't know if that is the elusive third way, but you can call it that if you want.

Note

[1] This chapter was initially presented at a seminar sponsored by the Smith Institute at 11 Downing Street on 20 May 1998. It was subsequently published in 1998 by the Smith Institute as a volume entitled *Equality and the modern economy*, edited by Wilf Stevenson. It is reproduced here by permission of the Smith Institute.

FIFTEEN

The new welfare

Bob Holman

Introduction

When William Beveridge published his famous Report in 1942, I was an evacuee. Eventually I returned home to the new welfare state Britain. It meant economic security for our family and it meant that I could be its first member to go to grammar school and university. I am grateful to Beveridge.

The new welfare

As a young man, Beveridge lived at Toynbee Hall and worked in the East End of London. Yet his Report said little about deprived areas. Its focus was on families and individuals, not neighbourhoods.

Today poverty is concentrated into 3,000 very deprived locations as identified by the Social Exclusion Unit. They are characterised by high unemployment, low incomes, poor health and drug abuse. I live in one of them, Easterhouse in Glasgow.

Yet not all is gloom. Within these same areas is a new form of welfare, one overlooked by Beveridge. I refer to neighbourhood groups or local community projects. These are activities which arise from within the areas not from outside. They are controlled by and run by residents. Examples are food co-ops, credit unions, youth clubs, community cafes, play schemes, second-hand furniture stores, community transport, and so on. According to the Community Development Foundation they have over two million participants.

Neighbourhood groups are significant for these reasons. First, they can *modify the effects of poverty*. They can sell cheap food, provide modestly priced holidays, ensure credit at low interest rates.

Second, *they support families*. Parents under stress can immediately turn to projects where they know and trust the staff. I am associated with a project call FARE (Family Action in Rogerfield and Easterhouse), which is based in five flats which became hard-to-let when drugs deaths occurred within them. Two of its 20-year-olds were asked on TV why they had not got into crime and drugs. They replied that the project had offered them clubs and sports as alternatives to gang life on the streets.

Third, they represent *a new kind of welfare*. It is not private welfare geared to making profit. It is not central government welfare which is often handicapped by bureaucracy. It is not local government welfare in which professionals from outside commute in to visit clients. Rather it is neighbourhood welfare in which staff and volunteers from the area serve their neighbours.

Fourth, *they strengthen participants*. In the book *Faith in the poor* (Holman, 1998), residents of Easterhouse write about themselves. A major theme is that they have grown in confidence when they became involved. Carol was a volatile lone mother with her child in care. She started to help at a lunch club and a food co-op. When she was elected chair of the latter, she said it was the first time she had ever been shown respect. As she found a purpose so her self-image was transformed. She won back her child and is now a respected community activist. She wrote "I've been supported and now I can support others".

Neighbourhood projects are run by low-income people in poor areas. Often they are in local authorities who cannot make grants to them. The hope must be that government will find a way of backing local projects. If not, here is a suggestion. Poor areas pay proportionately more into the National Lottery. Let all their lottery expenditure be immediately ploughed back into their areas for distribution among their projects. It would lead to more local jobs, better services and an enhanced neighbourhood spirit. A new welfare run by needy people for needy people.

References

Beveridge, Lord William (1942) *Social insurance and allied services*, Cmnd 6404, London: HMSO.

Holman, B. (1998) *Faith in the poor*, Oxford: Lion Publishing.

Section 3
Responses

SIXTEEN

A poor press? Media reception of the Beveridge Lecture

Simon Cross and Peter Golding

Good news is not always no news. When the Beveridge Report was published in December 1942 it met a big and largely enthusiastic press. Providing a warm uplift to the air of optimism coming from allied victories in North Africa, the promise of a better tomorrow turned the report into a best seller. The Stationery Office put 70,000 copies on sale on 2 December, and with queues running around the block, had sold out by lunchtime. Soon, over 600,000 copies were sold, and the 'people's William' was a national hero (Golding and Middleton, 1982, p 206). Page after page of detailed summary and analysis appeared in the broadsheets, *The Express* announced on its front page that 'Beveridge Tells How to Abolish Want'; the BBC broadcast details in 22 languages; and Beveridge's aide, Frank Pakenham (later Lord Longford), recalled in his memoir, "In my own experience I can recall no burst of acclamation remotely resembling it" (Pakenham, 1953, p 26).

Of course, enthusiasm in the coalition government for this full-blooded promotion was, at best, mixed. Attempts to damp down publicity were only reversed at the last minute, a change of direction perhaps prompted by the need to counter Goebbels' promise of a new European order. For two months the government remained silent in response, but the press (with the exception of *The Daily Telegraph*) "behaved as though it fell only slightly short of the millennium" (Addison, 1977, p 26). The Report, said *The Times*, was "a masterly exposition of the ways and means whereby the fact and fear of involuntary poverty can be speedily abolished altogether" (*The Times*, 2 December 1942, p 5).

Fifty-seven years later, the Prime Minster's Beveridge Lecture, recognising that no such 'speedy' outcome had arrived, added a further 20 years to the forecast, but received nothing like the same attention given to Beveridge, one of Mr Blair's 'lexicon of political heroes'. In assessing the media response to the Lecture we must recognise four realities: poverty is not news, poverty policy is rarely news, poverty is insistently understood in popular debate to be absolute not relative, and if poverty policy is to become news it is only through its contribution to political discord.

Ironically, just a couple of months after the Lecture, the Prime Minster was the speaker at the annual dinner of the Newspaper Society. Taking the opportunity to lambaste the press for its inadequate support during the conflict in Kosovo, Mr Blair suggested ruminatively, that "This is the media age, the era of 24-hour news, in which events are subject to instant and relentless analysis and commentary". If only! This speech, like the Beveridge Lecture, was scarcely and selectively reported. In this chapter we assess the media reporting of the Beveridge Lecture in the few days after it was delivered.

If the importance of an event is measured by the amount of attention given to it by television news, then the 1999 Beveridge Lecture was not an important event. Indeed, the Prime Minister's speech at Toynbee Hall was, in televisual terms at least, a non-story. In ITN's newly revamped early evening news programme at 6.30pm the speech was reported in an item lasting just less than two minutes, placed fourth in the bulletin. It was then dropped from ITN's final news programme at 11pm. The BBC's two main evening news programmes (BBC1's 9 O'Clock News and BBC2's Newsnight) both ignored the event completely. Not quite "instant and relentless analysis and commentary".

The general absence of television news coverage of the Beveridge Lecture says much about the way in which poverty policy does not become news. It is not simply that a speech on welfare policy reform by *any* political leader is dull and intrinsically non-newsworthy (consider how much broadcast news coverage is given to speeches at party conferences). It is, rather, that in the absence of a clearly defined party political dimension, news editors and journalists are inclined to ask 'what's the story?'

The national daily press gave Blair's speech fairly wide coverage, though with varying degrees of prominence across both the tabloids and the broadsheets. Table 1 shows where main news reports appeared within the national press and the column inches given to reportage of the Prime Minister's Beveridge Lecture.

Table 1: Press coverage of the 1999 Beveridge Lecture by page and column inch

Title	Page number	Column inches
The Mirror* (18 March)	1&2	54
The Mirror (19 March)	7	57
Daily Mail	2	12.5
The Sun	2	2
Daily Star	2	2.5
The Express	17	36
Daily Telegraph	8	62.5
The Guardian	10	73
The Times	12	42
Financial Times	8	22.5
The Independent	2	4.5
The Sunday Telegraph (21/3/99)	41	23

Note: *The Mirror* covered the Prime Minister's speech in its issue dated 18 March. All other press coverage of the speech is from newspapers dated 19 March.

As Table 1 shows, only *The Mirror* gave the Prime Minister's Beveridge Lecture front-page coverage (though it shared its 'exclusive' access to the content of Blair's speech with news of Liz Hurley's £2m salary for her next film role). On the day of the actual speech, however, its front page led with the story of the accidental death of puppeteer Rod Hull. It relegated a follow-up piece on child poverty to page 7. No other paper even gave the speech front-page exposure. The *Daily Star's* and *The Sun's* coverage both appeared on page 2, and each reported the speech in the space of two column inches (both less than 90 words). The *Daily Mail's* report was also to be found on page 2 but stretched to 12.5 column inches. By contrast, *The Express* gave the speech substantially more coverage, but its report only appeared on page 17, opposite a slightly larger advertisement for a national hotel chain.

If Blair's speech failed to make front-page news in the tabloids, it fared little better in the broadsheets. Thus, *The Independent's* report of the speech was its main 'Home News' item on page 2, albeit as an addendum to another story about Gordon Brown's plans to tax Child Benefit. *The Guardian*, meanwhile, gave the speech significantly more coverage, placing its report within its specialist 'Policy and Politics' section on page 10. Similarly, *The Times* also reported the speech in its 'Politics and Government' section on page 12. *The Daily Telegraph's* report was situated on page 8, alongside an accompanying commentary from the paper's Home Affairs Editor. The *Financial Times* also placed its report on page 8, within its 'National News' section, along with a short accompanying article entitled 'Changing Definitions of Poverty'. It is also worth noting that none of the Sunday newspapers (both tabloids and broadsheets) covered the Prime Minister's speech as a news item. The only commentary was that given by Auberon Waugh in his column in *The Sunday Telegraph*.

This was, of course, at the height of the conflict in Kosovo. The major news of the day, however, was elsewhere. The murder and funeral of Northern Ireland lawyer Rose Nelson took a lot of the limelight. In the increasingly tabloidised *The Times* it was 'Millennium Dome Tickets Costing Up to £20', and 'Times Tipsters 3001-1 treble'. *The Sun*, like *The Mirror*, led on Rod Hull, the deceased begetter of Emu (not a story on Brussels financial manoeuvring). By Sunday the big news in *The Express* was Prince Charles' plea to 'Cut Back Please, Granny', while *The Mail on Sunday* had 'Fayed's £30,000 gift to Tebbitt,' and *The Mirror*, 'Secret £20,000 of Lewis Fight judge'. The *Sunday People* led with '£1 Million Lottery Winner Marries Down and Out' (so poverty crept in at the margins), and the *News of the World* did not disappoint with 'Girl Who Knows What MP Did in Brothel'. The slice of life which is the raw material for the news machine was the usual mix of celebrity, calamity, and frivolity which have become its staple fare. But of the apocalyptic promise to end child poverty there was little to be seen.

By contrast, the clippings files bulged just two months later when the government found itself besieged by its own backbenchers over plans to cut eligibility to disability benefits. The story was the backbench revolt, as the honeymoon balloon to be so punctured by the subsequent European election results, begun to wilt as the press began to scent a real 'Labour split'. 'Biggest Revolt Against Blair Over Benefit Cuts' (*Daily Mail*, 17 May) followed by a feature in the same paper by Graeme Wilson on 'Ministers Running Scared on Benefit Cutbacks' set the tone. With the vote in the House, the headline was 'Blair's 67 Refuseniks' (*Daily Mail*, 20 May). In *The Mirror* the story focused on 'Defiant Social Security Secretary Alistair Darling' standing firm, under the headline 'Darling's Anger at Revolt on Disabled'. *The Guardian* reported that 'Ministers Struggle to Limit Revolt on Welfare' (19 May) and that 'Labour Rattled by Welfare Revolt' (front page, 18 May). As we have shown elsewhere, in examining reporting of the poll tax, it is the politics not the policy which makes the headlines (Deacon and Golding, 1994).

Unlike the Blair Lecture, here was a story with real red meat to tempt the feeding frenzy of political reporting.

However, one aspect of the speech was certainly considered newsworthy by all the daily newspapers. Consider Blair's opening remarks at Toynbee Hall:

> **"Today I want to talk to you about a great challenge: how we make the welfare state popular again. How we restore public trust and confidence in a welfare state that 50 years ago was acclaimed but today has so many people wanting to bury it. I will argue that the only road to 'a popular welfare state' is radical welfare reform. And I will set out our historic aim that ours is the first generation to end child poverty forever, and it will take a generation. It is a 20-year mission but I believe it can be done."**

The 20-year target inevitably caught such headlines as there were, surprisingly crowding out any focus on the more immediate, and in many ways more dramatic and significant declaration that the government's "plans will start by lifting 700,000 children out of poverty by the end of the Parliament". Reports picked up the longer-term, messianic, theme, while the specific shorter-term target received less comment. Words such as 'target' (*The Guardian*, 19 March; *Daily Mail*, 19 March), 'mission' (*Financial Times*, 19 March), *The Daily Telegraph*, 19 March), 'war' and 'crusade' (*Daily Star*, 19 March), 'wipe out' (*The Mirror*, 19 March) and 'pledge' (*The Express*, 19 March; *The Sun*, 19 March) emotively conveyed a Prime Minister giving notice that child poverty is to become a thing of the past. Such a reaction to ending child poverty would not have been surprising even in the absence of deliberate spin. But as we shall see, however, despite (and in some cases perhaps even because of) evident government spin, not every commentator reacted to Blair's speech with uniform praise.

Reporting the mission – the real story

We begin, though, with *The Mirror*, since it was in that traditional bastion of Old Labour support where New Labour spin was most apparent. On the day of the actual speech its 'exclusive' front-page headline voiced Blair's unequivocal determination to end child poverty: "I'll End All Child Poverty In 20 Years [sic]". Indeed, its advance knowledge of Blair's statement was enough for the paper's editorial to declare that "now its end is in sight" (18 March, p 6). But any suggestion that the Prime Minister alone might bring an end to child poverty is dashed, however, as *The Mirror's* editorial commentary subsequently makes clear: "This is a wonderful ambition and is not based on wild promises. Mr Blair does not pretend to have a magic wand which can make things come right instantly. *The process will take 20 years, so some children will still suffer. But it is better to be honest than make cruel pledges that cannot be fulfilled*". He will do it by changing the nation's attitude to the welfare state (p 6, original emphasis).

But herein lies the political rub. According to *The Mirror*, ending child poverty will only be realised via reform of one of Labour's greatest political monuments – the welfare state. The paper's Chief Political Commentator, Paul Routledge, explained: "In tonight's speech [sic], Tony Blair will seek to change the face of the welfare state – away from the image of laziness and fraud, so it is a force for progress. As a first-generation child of the welfare state, I welcome his initiative" (the Lecture was, in fact, given at 12 noon). After giving his stamp of approval Routledge's approach then pivots on Blair's notion of 'popular welfare' as a 'hand-up' ("Labour is spending £6 billion more on lifting children out of poverty in this parliament's lifetime") rather than a 'hand-out' ("The future lies with working people. Only we can make it work, because it is the product of our labour and taxes"). Consequently, he is able to declare the Labour government's measures to improve the benefits system as "showing that it still has its roots among the people".

The day after the speech *The Mirror*, in fact, went 'among the people'. By doing so they located the contemporary face of child poverty in Britain in the form of 12-year-old Tommy Keating. Alongside a three-quarter page photograph of Tommy (also included were two inset photographs of his parents and his bedroom), readers were informed that:

> **He's pale, sickly and underfed. His home is cold, damp and squalid. He rarely goes to school. His mother spends her time drinking cheap cider. He begins every day wandering the streets. He ends each day in despair. (*The Mirror*, 19 March, p 7)**

The title of *The Mirror's* case study of Tommy's life is 'Poor Kid'. The ambiguity in the headline derives both from the reality of his miserable, poverty-ridden, existence and his inability to conceive of a life better than the one he presently inhabits: "The saddest fact of all is that Tommy has no idea how much better life can be. He has never known anything else". But, as the following passage from the 'Poor Kid' article also reveals, it was not the only reality that the paper sought to convey:

> **Tommy is one of 4.6 million children in Britain who Premier Tony Blair pledged yesterday to help in a bid to wipe out child poverty within 20 years.** *But unless he is helped now it will be too late.* **(p 7, our emphasis)**

Perhaps having had time to reflect on the Prime Minister's 20-year timetable, *The Mirror* was now more circumspect about what might be achieved in the short term. Certainly, its editorial tone was less bullish than the previous day:

> **Anyone who thinks Tony Blair hasn't got a fight on his hands ridding Britain of child poverty should read the story of Tommy Keating.**

And when it comes to fighting child poverty, the paper understood that long-term objectives sometimes have to override short-term solutions:

> **Some critics may complain that Mr Blair's 20 year timetable is too long. But the crucial thing is to end poverty. Posturing about being able to do it overnight would be pointless.** *It may come too late for Tommy. But everyone who is saved will bring nearer the day when no child lives like him.* **(p 6, emphasis in original)**

Here, *The Mirror* took issue with Martin Barnes, Director of the Child Poverty Action Group (CPAG). In a short accompanying commentary to the 'Poor Kid' article, Barnes argued that, "The Government should be more radical. There needs to be a redistribution of wealth. The target should be to end child poverty in 10 years, not 20" (19 March, p 7). Thus, despite the sarcasm over his timetable to end child poverty 'overnight', the paper's point is clear: CPAG's own 10-year timetable is flawed compared with Blair's 20-year timetable. Thus Barnes' complaint about the 20-year timetable becomes one of simple 'posturing'.

The Guardian's main report of the Beveridge Lecture also acknowledged criticism of Blair's speech (particularly from shadowy figures 'on Mr Blair's left'). But on the specific issue of ending child poverty its editorial commentary could not resist injecting a more sardonic tone:

> **Nirvana beckons. The Prime Minister promised yesterday to end child poverty within the next 20 years. The NSPCC earlier this week promised to end child cruelty within a similar time frame. What a week! Oh to be in Britain in 2019.**

One suspects that Downing Street can live with such biting sarcasm, especially given the paper's cautious but optimistic welcome to the setting of a 20-year target to end child poverty. However, *The Guardian* did eventually raise some points of contention concerning the *means* by which welfare reform is to be achieved:

> **Some crucial questions remain unanswered (like which mechanisms will be used? and how will poverty be defined?), several contradictions ignored (both universal and means-tested benefits were embraced), and the toughest decision ducked: you cannot eliminate poverty without embracing the one policy which ministers refuse to acknowledge: redistribution.**

The Guardian subsequently orchestrated a series of specialist responses to Blair's speech in its Society section the following week (31 March). Alone among national dailies (with the exception of *The Mirror's* invitation to the CPAG), *The Guardian* gave a 'right of reply' to Blair's Beveridge speech. The paper invited three experts in social policy (David Piachaud, Ruth Lister and Bob Holman; see also Chapter 17), with whom the Prime Minister had, as the speech acknowledges, consulted before he gave his Beveridge Lecture, to respond to the realism of Blair's goal of ending child poverty within 20 years. Not surprisingly, perhaps, their points of engagement with Blair's speech differed as each writer sought to establish their own agenda on child poverty as well as outline their individual views on welfare reform.

Despite their differences of perspective, however, each writer acknowledged the impact of recent Labour budget changes (on rises in Income Support rates for children under 11, on the Working Families Tax Credit) in helping to promote or alleviate (depending on viewpoint) child poverty. Moreover, each used their allotted space to advance their own 'alternative' proposals for ending child poverty. They included: reducing income inequalities; providing research-based assessment of the (in)adequacy of children's benefits; establishing a Poverty Unit within the Cabinet Office. Thus, while *The Guardian's* initial editorial response had been to only scratch the surface of what Blair actually meant by ending child poverty, its Society pages were more able to address the contested range of possibilities that his statement gives rise to.

Poverty – hard times to new times

Much of the commentary and analysis prompted by the speech revisited the familiar debate about absolute and relative poverty. Much of the press, like public opinion when tapped, prefers its poverty to be visible and abject, preferably signified by snotty-nosed street urchins in rags. The growing gap between high and low incomes is another matter. The weekly business and politics magazine, *The Economist*, asked "what does Mr Blair mean by ending child poverty?" (*The Economist*, 4 March, p 32) and immediately answered that "he is careful not to say". Their interest in asking this question, though, derives from the criticism it allows vis-à-vis the Labour government's strategy of increasing the levels of means-tested benefits. Consequently, they reminded readers that:

> **Labour's own definitions of poverty have changed over time. In opposition, the party chanted 'the rich are getting richer while the poor are getting poorer'. Labour equated the poor either with the bottom tenth of the population or with people on means-tested benefits, below the poverty line. (p 32)**

and that

> **In government, Labour has discovered the drawbacks of this approach. Raising the levels of means-tested benefits increases the numbers of people who qualify for them. And one of the government's deliberate strategies had been to do exactly that. On Labour's old definition, this perversely increases poverty. (p 32)**

For *The Economist*, then, the hard theoretical problem of defining the meaning of poverty gives rise to even harder practical implications for government policies designed to counter it. Furthermore, while it agrees that "bigger welfare payments ... help today's poor children" it also suggests that the longer-term demographic reality of poorer families having more children than richer ones makes the total eradication of poverty "harder still". But, as it dryly points out, "this is likely to worry future administrations more than it worries Mr Blair. Not even he can expect still to be Prime Minister in 20 years' time" (p 32).

The meaning of poverty also taxed Philip Johnston, Home Affairs Editor of *The Daily Telegraph*. By asking "what did Mr Blair mean when he said 'our historic aim is to be the first generation to end child poverty?'" (*The Daily Telegraph*, 19 March), he sought to pin-point exactly what Blair *did not* mean:

> **He clearly did not mean the grinding poverty of the mid-19th century, graphically depicted in *Mayhew's London* or by Dickens. Nor could he have meant the privations of pre-war Britain, whose inner-city squalor can still be attested to by so many alive today. (p 8)**

For Johnston, then, the 'grinding poverty' of Dickens' era is the genuine article. But whether he was referring to the literary or (more likely) televisual Dickens, Johnston does not make clear. What is more certain, however, is that contemporary definitions of child poverty are susceptible to accusations that things are not now as bad as they were in Dickens' time. Dickens provides a point of reference too for *The Mirror*, in an editorial which nonetheless pointed out that:

> **It is 150 years since Charles Dickens opened the eyes of the British people to child poverty. So much has changed since then. Yet still too many children live in misery. They do not have to cope with the slums and rags of Dickens's time, but they still go hungry and grow up without hope. *It is a scandal that such poverty exists in the midst of the plenty that most Britons enjoy.* (p 6, emphasis in original)**

But while it cautiously established our distance and our difference from the child poverty of Dickens' era, *The Mirror* is nevertheless certain that "in the midst of plenty", child poverty still exists. In Johnston's view, however, things are not quite so straightforward. Referring to the number of people cited by Blair in his Beveridge Lecture as living in poverty, he exhumes the familiar argument against relative poverty measures:

> **Mr Blair spoke yesterday against a background assumption that 14 million people in Britain are now living in poverty or at its margins. The reason is that poverty has been redefined to the point where it can never be abolished, let alone within 20 years. (p 8)**

Johnston then corrects the Prime Minster's terminology by suggesting he is, in fact, discussing "inequality not want". He goes on: "There is a legitimate debate to be had over the extent to which the fruits of economic advancement are being shared out across the populace". However, Johnston's benevolence on this point belies a much more mischievous aim. In his opening comments Johnston scathingly noted Blair's reluctance to answer when recently asked in the House of Commons if he considered himself a socialist ("the Prime Minister managed to remember that his party still defended itself as 'democratic socialist...'"). He warmed to this theme again in his closing remarks in order to taunt the seriousness of Blair's desire to tackle poverty:

> **If … what he really wants is to eradicate inequalities, then why does he not use the instrument beloved of old-style redistributionists – the tax system? As Mr Blair's Commons questioner asked: is he a socialist or not? (p 8)**

Although his question is left hanging in the air, Johnston's headline, in fact, provides an answer: "All Things Being Equal, He's A Socialist". Thus, while centre-left commentators like Routledge find it easy to accept that child poverty exists, it is ironic that an avowedly right-wing commentator like Johnston is more easily able to introduce the question of redistributive tax policies into public debate about welfare reform.

In a short piece accompanying its main report of the Beveridge Lecture, *The Times* also noted changing definitions of poverty: "The definition of poverty has changed significantly over the last 60 years from having barely enough to eat to having enough to buy cigarettes and a second-hand television". The wistful tone of distaste for this generous redefinition is unmistakable. It was left to the paper's editorial, however, to inject a dose of political realism into Blair's public statement:

> **His call for an end to child poverty in Britain within 20 years is an objective on a vastly different scale from that of reducing class sizes. There is much to be said in favour of deadlines in political life especially when the aim in itself may be universally acclaimed as laudable. It is less certain whether that applies when, as in this case, the timescale is so long and the terminology involved distinctly uncertain. (p 23)**

The Times' editorial also sketched a historical resumé of this century's Liberal and Labour politicians who, like Blair, had also pledged an end to poverty. The Asquith government in particular, emerged with honour, because:

> **It mixed public and private provision and recognised that there were limits to what could be imposed through centralised bureaucracy. Much was achieved and the worst aspects of national squalor banished. But poverty itself was certainly not eradicated. (p 23)**

The substance of Blair's commitment to end child poverty is then assessed for its political significance, and there finds some comfortingly tough elements to commend:

> **The substance of the Prime Minister's speech was somewhat more significant than the soundbite which accompanied it. Mr Blair outlined an approach that combats social exclusion through work, favours action against the cultural as well as economic aspects of poverty and concedes a larger role for the private sector. Although entitled 'the Beveridge Lecture' his words were closer in spirit to those that inspired Mr Asquith rather than Mr Attlee. (p 23)**

While *The Times* sees through the soundbite aspects of Blair's speech, and remains unconvinced about his aim to end child poverty (the editorial's title, 'Always With Us', confirms this), the link between Blair and Asquith and *not Beveridge* is seen as crucial: "It is ... the factor that offers him the opportunity to affect real change [for welfare reform], if not on the ambitious scale of ending child poverty that he suggested" (p 23).

The Times was not alone in drawing attention to Blair's description of himself as political heir to Beveridge. The *Financial Times* politely noted that "Tony Blair's claim to be heir to William Beveridge, founder of the Welfare State, is premature to say the least" (p 17). More pointedly, however, it argued that Blair's aim of ending child poverty "may divert attention from the hard choices in reforming welfare" (p 17). Drawing on Blair's own assessment in his Beveridge Lecture, the paper agreed that:

> **... the social safety net established 50 years ago could hardly be expected to meet the very different needs of the 21st**

century. There are now far greater proportions of pensioners, single mothers and women at work, for example. (p 17)

It then located exactly where in the 'social safety net' that "very different needs of the 21st century" were most apparent:

The problem in most industrial societies is that as universal benefits are extended to create a genuine freedom from want, taxation has been applied to those on low pay rates. Strong disincentives have resulted. (p 17)

Having thus identified the 'problem' of universal benefits breeding taxation disincentives, it then advised on how to overcome problems caused by the latter through more closely targeting the former:

The two main ways of achieving this are to put greater emphasis on means testing and to impose tough conditions, such as those that apply to the young unemployed under the new deal. Both can be justified, but they amount effectively to an ending of the universal insurance against poverty and sickness as envisaged by Beveridge. They also create new problems of equity and social acceptability. (p 17)

In the *Financial Times'* opinion, then, the Labour government faces a hard choice. Reform of the benefits/welfare system can be achieved but may incur a high political cost: "For example, a better system of housing benefits, which Mr Blair says is next on the agenda, will create large numbers of losers among Labour voters" (p 17).

Blair's speech provoked the considerable ire of Auberon Waugh. Writing in *The Sunday Telegraph* (21 March) Waugh entered the debate on child poverty armed with a particularly heavy arsenal of sarcasm, hobby horses, and personal invective towards Blair. And as the following passages illustrate, he was in no mood to take prisoners:

How does he propose to abolish child poverty without abolishing adult poverty at the same time? One might easily decide that Mr Blair, far from demonstrating his idealism, is showing himself to be a fraud. Of course Mr Blair would have to abolish all poverty before he could abolish child poverty. The promise to abolish poverty has been the refrain

> **of every crooked demagogue since politics began, and nobody
> would have believed him. (p 1)**

> **There is something ... a little bit odd about his choice of
> child poverty as the thing to abolish. What have children got
> to do with it? Perhaps he is guilty of nothing worse than
> pandering to the nauseating and slightly mad sentimentality
> about children which is such a feature of British society at
> the present time. One wonders that this sentimentality, which
> is not shared by any of our European neighbours, applies to
> children only in the abstract sense. (p 41)**

Waugh touches on some controversial issues including, as the first passage
shows, the difficult question of how one might abolish child poverty
without simultaneously ending *adult* poverty. Indeed, by asking "What
have children got to do with it?", Waugh, in inimitable style, noted the
likely political consequence of an equivalent commitment by Blair to
end *all* poverty:

> **Perhaps Tony Blair, despite having three children of his own,
> genuinely subscribes to these feelings about 'kids' in the
> abstract sense. Even so, one suspects there is an element of
> political calculation in his promise to end child poverty,
> knowing perfectly well that if he promised to abolish all
> poverty we would laugh in his face and show him the door.
> (p 41)**

Notwithstanding the heavy sarcasm, this is an important point. Perhaps
Waugh even had one or two political casualties in mind but was discrete
enough not to name names. *The Economist,* incidentally, was less
charitable:

> **In the past politicians who talked about poverty played with
> fire. Remember John Moore? Few do. In the 1980s Mr
> Moore was tipped as Margaret Thatcher's successor as Tory
> leader – until, as social-security secretary, he made a speech
> announcing the end of poverty. The resulting uproar finished
> his career. (*The Economist*, 3 April, p 32)**

Quite so. And as Waugh himself suggests, Blair knows 'perfectly well'
that some comments from politicians go down better with the public

than others. Indeed, it is precisely the "political calculation in his promise to end child poverty" that so incenses him and provokes an almost Malthusian anger:

> **He says there are 14 million people living in poverty in this country. Well, of course there are, when poverty is defined as living on less than half the national average wage. Similarly, he may decide there are six million children living in poverty. The only way to change that would be to stop the poor having children, but he has not suggested that. (p 41)**

But Waugh's principal cynicism is reserved for Blair's talk of a 'historic mission' to end child poverty. Thus, it is "no more than a childish boast, a measure of his self-importance". Likening it to a "new form of child abuse" Waugh then points to the way politicians routinely use children to further their political aims:

> **The appeal for more expenditure on child poverty represents no more than an appeal for more government spending. That is what politicians enjoy doing more than anything else, and that is why children are such a boon to them. (p 41)**

At this point, and with the finesse of a bruising heavyweight boxer, Waugh moves in to deliver his final, knockout, blow:

> **Even welfare has become something of a dirty word, as Mr Blair pointed out in his Beveridge lecture, when applied to the dependency culture of the North of England. So everything has to be put on the children. Nobody dares sneer at the idea of child poverty. (p 41)**

Perhaps conscious of the Prime Minister's own North-East constituency, Waugh recycles a familiar conservative myth of the 'idle North'. Indeed, he need only mention the 'North of England' in order to set in motion an unwritten chain of negative associations of Northerners as 'workshy', 'lazy', or 'scroungers'. The only difficulty here, however, is that Blair's comments about a 'dependency culture' contained *nothing* about 'the North of England'. Ever an eye for entertaining, but also misinforming, his readers, Waugh had conveniently added his own geographical prejudice to a carefully selected element of the Prime Minister's speech.

Writing in *The Independent's Friday Review*, Deborah Orr did comment on the 700,000 target, but pointed out that, "While New Labour asserts that these measures will lift 700,000 children out of poverty, it is estimated that a staggering 3.9 million will still be left below the poverty line." Orr's response to the Beveridge Lecture includes thoughts on what else might be achieved during the next 20 years other than eradicating child poverty. Among her proposals is an equitable approach to parenting which centres on fathers having greater domestic involvement in a child's early years. She also suggests a more 'revolutionary' approach to caring for our children which includes "providing for our parenting years privately ... with parent plans supplementing pension plans". As she puts it:

> **This is the revolution we should be planning over the next 20 years. Child poverty we can eradicate by the end of the next Labour government. Only money can stop poverty. Radical reform should be directed at creating far more complex kinds of change. (The Independent Friday Review, p 5)**

Visualising poverty: from the playground to the bedroom

One of the consistent themes of contemporary critics of the poverty lobby is the distinction between 'genuine' and 'non-genuine' poverty, a close parallel to the deserving and undeserving poor. In a number of the commentaries discussed above we have seen how some writers draw upon this distinction, not least to reject calls for financial responses to alleviating, if not poverty, then 'Want'. (It is also worth noting that some commentators also acknowledge that poverty has improved but that things should be better.) It is significant, therefore, that in those reports of the Beveridge Lecture that did accept the need for government action to alleviate child poverty (in some cases, having first argued about the meaning of the term) visual images play an important role in grounding exactly what it is that child poverty *looks like*.

Deborah Orr's substantial review of Blair's speech ('For the Sake of Our Children', *The Independent Friday Review*, p 5) carried a particularly striking photograph of young children playing among the wreckage of an abandoned car, all of whom appear encased within a drab housing estate located underneath a dark, brooding, skyline. Its highly stylised representation of child poverty as an evil and malevolent force residing in the margins of decent, civilised society is reinforced by the accompanying question/caption, 'Does Britain suffer from "kiddie apartheid", with "nice" middle-class children being kept away from the "bogey-kiddies"?' As we have seen above, *The Independent* is clear about the answer to this question. Here is the underclass incarnate.

The Express also carried a picture of three young children playing, set against a drab landscape of concrete tower blocks. It was accompanied by the headline:'Wanted:A Better Place For Children To Play'. Ironically, it appeared on the same page as an advertisement for a national hotel chain. Thus, almost diametrically opposite the children's picture was another image, this time of a young couple with wide smiles and sparkling white teeth. Underneath was the caption:'Leisure Clubs With Swimming Pools At Most Hotels'. No doubt leisure clubs with swimming pools are a better place for poor children to play, but are probably not what *The Express* had in mind.

Other papers provide an alternative picture of child poverty. *The Mirror, The Economist* and *The Guardian* each presented a picture of a child alone in a bedroom devoid of the normal accoutrements of a young life: pictures, posters and toys. Via this image we penetrate an 'other' world, a subterranean world of child poverty and abandoned hope. For *The Economist*, it simply confirmed the economic challenge facing present and future politicians ("... the government wants to encourage parents to provide for their children through work, rather than relying on the state"). But for *The Mirror*, concerned with documenting the minutiae of Tommy's drab existence, it means much more: "After rolling out of the single bed he shares with his brother he starts his day with a cannabis spliff then strolls the street in despair, sometimes not returning until 3am". A small inset picture of Tommy lying in bed confirms the utter hopelessness of his life.

Conclusion: poverty and public debate

Poverty is not news, but Prime Ministerial set piece speeches often are. Reporting of the Beveridge Lecture failed to capture the headlines despite its apocalyptic promises, not least because it did not resonate with the usual accompaniments of poverty news, namely crime (fraud and its repression), and political wrangling (as subsequently provoked by the disability benefit proposals). It did, however, readily unearth familiar questions in popular commentary about the nature of poverty (real, meaning absolute, as distinct from unreal, meaning relative), and its iconography (the requisite squalor which true poverty should display to remove our doubts and uncertainties). In this it fell into a familiar pattern of poverty news in the 1990s (Golding, forthcoming).

In fact the speech said surprisingly little about benefits and almost nothing about income – the 'modern welfare state' is about education, unemployment, drugs, responsibility, enabling, ending the systematic encouragement of fraud, and private/public partnerships (Chapter 17). Its very New Labour message, 'if you work hard you will not be in poverty', offers no challenge to press commentators focusing on what is wrong rather than right with a comprehensive and adequate benefits system. Its proudest boast is that "Since we came to government we have cut the real growth of social security spending by almost 1% a year. In our first two years we have spent over £5 billion less than the previous government planned for." Despite the relative absence of reporting, and the substantially sceptical commentary on the substance of the speech, the net effect of media response was largely reinforcement of the skewed character of poverty news with which we have long been familiar.

References

Addison, P. (1997) *The road to 1945*, London: Quartet Books.

Deacon, D. and Golding, P. (1994) *Taxation and representation: The media, political communication and the poll tax*, Luton: John Libbey.

Golding, P. (forthcoming) '"Thinking the unthinkable", social security and the news media in the 1990s', in B. Franklin (ed) *Misleading messages: The media, misrepresentation, and social policy*, London: Routledge.

Golding, P. and Middleton, S. (1982) *Images of welfare: Press and public attitudes to poverty*, Oxford: Martin Robertson.

Pakenham, F. (1953) *Born to believe*, London: Jonathan Cape.

SEVENTEEN

Dimensions of the debate: reflections on the Beveridge Lecture

Robert Walker

It was the commitment to end child poverty within 20 years that captured media interest in the days following the Beveridge Lecture. Before 1 May 1997, poverty had been a proscribed word in official circles for a political generation and the idea that government should or, indeed, could, do anything about it was also ridiculed. Tony Blair not only promises to eradicate child poverty, he commits himself to a timetable that could conceivably fall within an unbroken spell of Labour rule. This new policy goal was not chosen at random, it is consistent with the concept of social justice that lies at the foundation of Blair's vision of social welfare.

Less remarked upon, but of real importance, is the emphasis given in Blair's Lecture to transforming welfare from 'a term of abuse' into something 'popular'. A necessary pre-condition for achieving the goal of eradicating childhood poverty, it could also have profound implications for both the delivery of welfare and the status accorded to welfare recipients. Welfare might become the instrument for fostering social cohesion through the language of social inclusion in the way that Beveridge foresaw it as part of post-war reconstruction.

The continuing legacy of Beveridge is indeed remarkable. Beveridge was engaged in the policy arena for so long, in so many capacities and offered so many insights, some of them contradictory (as Tony Atkinson affirms), that almost any policy prescription could be presented as being either 'new' or 'old' Beveridge. Nevertheless, Jose Harris, who knows more about Beveridge than anyone else, concludes that "the principles and assumptions woven into the fabric of the Beveridge Plan ... have a certain relevance – even an elective affinity - with some of the core ideas of New Labour".

But the Lecture is perhaps most notable, in this age of soundbites, for the opportunity afforded to assemble the concepts and principles that define New Labour's thinking and to apply them to a central policy concern, the future of welfare. As a consequence, much is learned about Blair's ideas on 'the Third Way', 'modernisation', the 'knowledge economy', 'social responsibility', 'welfare contracts' and 'social inclusion'.

Still greater depth of understanding comes from reading the Lecture alongside the ideas and insights of experts who are well aware of the history and challenges of the welfare state. Although generally committed to the aspirations of the centre-left, they offer a professional detachment that helps to inform Blair's analysis and, on occasion, to separate the desirable from the less desirable and the possible from the portentous. There is also interest in identifying which ideas Blair took up, and in what form, and those that he rejected.

The aim, therefore, in this final chapter is to elucidate the major areas of agreement and disagreement between Blair and the welfare experts, and among the experts themselves, with a view to defining the dimensions of the debate that is necessary if Blair's vision is to become a blueprint for the future.

Social justice

The concept of social justice lies at the heart of Blair's Lecture and of his vision of an evolving welfare state. An objective, rather than just a guiding principle of policy, Blair's conception of social justice is based on the concepts of decency, merit, mutual responsibility, fairness and 'timeless values', the application of which changes with the changing world. It provides "the basis for a community where everyone has a chance to succeed" and in which "power, wealth and opportunity will be in the hands of the many not the few".

Most, though not all, the contributors agree about the importance of merit, mutual responsibility and fairness. A concern with equality of outcome, once widespread on the centre-left, is replaced by a focus on equality of opportunity. Life chances should depend on merit and effort, not on birth. Simple redistribution that fails to take account of the reasons for people's financial circumstances, Le Grand argues, is likely to be socially unjust (not benefiting the indigent) and inefficient (because it penalises effort). Most people would therefore consider simple redistribution to be unfair. But, whereas a Thatcherite or classical liberal might respond with passive policies that ensure a person's freedom is not infringed, modern social democrats argue for proactive policies that enhance equality of opportunity. Redistribution is "redefined as the redistribution of life chances" (Giddens). Such policies promote positive freedom – "the freedom/ability to do things and having the appropriate resources and opportunities" (Plant) – and empowerment (Piachaud) – the ability to exploit opportunity. Social Democrats accept that government can and should interfere to ameliorate unjust market outcomes and to dismantle the discriminatory barriers that society so readily creates (Le Grand).

Le Grand suggests that this emphasis on promoting opportunity requires a shift in policy away from a reliance on benefits and taxation as the principal means of achieving social justice. This is clearly not a shift away from the Beveridge vision – since he sought to slay not one but five giants blocking the road to progress and reconstruction. Rather it may be a move away from those on the 'Old Left' that Blair believes "divorced economic efficiency from social justice" and sought to use the tax system as a primary mechanism of redistribution. The proactive policies that Blair emphasises include education, health reforms and measures to tackle 'social decay' as well as Welfare to Work. Likewise, Piachaud aspires to tackle the causes of social injustice: the lack of employment opportunities, education, training, rehabilitation and good quality housing upon which "independence and the opportunity to produce for oneself" depend. Kellner, who believes government should seek to promote equality of access above equality of opportunity, would go further and include equal membership rights to information, power, security and justice. Tackling social injustice on such a broad range of fronts emphasises the need for joined-up government and will in time provide a stringent test of its effectiveness.

Accompanying this proactive pursuit of enhanced opportunity is a demand for mutual responsibility. For Kellner, as much as for Blair, mutuality or 'mutualism' is about "the basic relationships between citizens, communities, employers and the state". "For a free society to flourish, the exercise of individual liberty requires the acknowledgement of mutual responsibility". Rather than responsibilities eroding rights, Piachaud suggests that they make rights sustainable. They bind citizens together in a protective fabric of self-interest and mutual support or, at the very least, demonstrate to the taxpayer that welfare is only available to those prepared to try to help themselves (Deacon).

Lest it be thought that the emphasis placed on responsibilities is new, Plant points out that the concept of an active and inclusive citizenry and the notion of autonomy have long been central to the social democratic ideal. Beveridge – as a Progressive Liberal – also constantly stressed that social policy should at all costs avoid people coming to expect "something for nothing" (Giddens). One danger, alluded to by

Walker and Lister, is that, unless sensitively handled, undue emphasis on obligation may create the incorrect impression that all welfare recipients would abuse the system unless forced to do otherwise.

There may be less consensus around the concept of decency: that citizens should be able to meet their needs for income, housing, health and education. One reason is that Blair is imprecise about the minimum thresholds that are to pass for decency. Labour's welfare reviews to date have failed, as Lister notes, to address the issue of adequacy or to develop a minimum income standard as suggested by the European Commission. While Labour has established a series of minima, with minimum income guarantees for pensioners and severely disabled people and, through the Working Families Tax Credit, for families in work, they have not been set with explicit reference to evidence on adequacy. Nor is the resultant minimum threshold universal in coverage. Also, most benefits[1] continue to be uprated in line with prices with the result that benefit recipients will fail to share in society's growing affluence (Hills). However, the issue of adequacy will presumably have to be addressed in the first poverty audit that is due to be published around the same time as this volume.

Finally, Blair envisages a concept of justice in which the application of such timeless values as decency, fairness, merit and mutual responsibility changes with changing times; hence, '*New* Labour' and modernisation.

Modernisation

Blair's Lecture reveals at least three dimensions to modernisation: practical, pragmatic and political. To take the practical first, the world is very different to what it was at the time of the Beveridge Report. Blair follows Hills' analysis on the changing position of women and the ageing society. But he shifts the emphasis when talking about the changed labour market and makes no reference to the growing affluence of our society or the developments set in train by Beveridge and the Attlee government. In this Blair is perhaps being pragmatic, using evidence of social change to legitimate a principled ideological position. Whereas Hills draws attention to increased inequality caused by globalisation that has decisively weakened the labour market position of the least skilled, Blair concludes that globalisation has undermined any prospect of full employment. This assumption, pivotal to the vision of Beveridge, Blair says, has "been completely broken down". Modern policies make no explicit mention of redistribution to address growing inequality in incomes, while macro-economic policy aims to ensure stability rather than boost labour demand.

Finally, modernisation is used politically in two ways. First, Blair emphasises the impotence of opposition both within and outside the Labour Party. The opposite of new is old and out of date. The 'Old Left', with its emphasis on redistribution and indifference to economic efficiency, is clearly not modern. Equally, modern policies have dumbfounded the Opposition – and "been less controversial than anticipated"[2], attracting opposition only from the 'usual suspects', including – one supposes – some social policy professors[3].

Second, Blair contrasts failure "to create a modern welfare state fit for the modern world" with Labour's aspirations and strategy. He cites Piachaud's condemnation of Conservative rule that created more poverty, more inequality, more dependency on means-tested benefits and more street homeless. The Conservatives were right about the importance of the market and greater competition but wrong, according to Blair, in their attempts merely to cut spending rather than to "tackle the fundamental weaknesses of the welfare state", and in their failure to modernise the welfare system.

Blair calls on Beveridge in support of his concept of modernisation. Like Atkinson he believes that Beveridge would have been profoundly irritated by any assumption that his policy solutions were permanent and for all time. Beveridge, like New Labour, was immensely careful and prudent in financial planning (Harris). He also refused to accept – as Blair accuses both the Old Left and the New Right of doing – that economic and social policy can be viewed in distinct compartments. Indeed, Blair believes that one of Beveridge's 'key insights' was his realisation that "the concept of social welfare had to fit economic policy". However, taken too literally this risks distortion. Beveridge did not view social policy simply as the handmaiden of the economy. Rather he exploited the potential symbiosis between economic and social policy. With this in mind, Atkinson acknowledges that the 21st century welfare state has to take full account of its impact on incentives for workers and employers but argues that labour market flexibility is not enough: there is a role for macro-economic policy in tacking poverty and social exclusion. He doubts, too, whether Beveridge would have concluded that globalisation and Britain's exposure to world markets had rendered meaningless the concept of the national welfare state. Moreover, Beveridge might well have perceived an obligation on Britain to promote the integration of social and economic policy at European level.

Popular welfare

Blair used the Beveridge Lecture to add the goal of making welfare popular to that of modernisation. This is clearly an apposite juxtaposition since the Beveridge Plan achieved unexpected mass popularity on a perhaps unique scale. The Plan reflected and required a very high degree of social solidarity that Harris believes "fitted the social reality of 1942 more than any earlier or later moment in history".

But Blair recognises – as do Lister, Toynbee and Walker – that in recent years welfare has become a term of abuse. It is too often perceived to be "the problem not the solution" associated with "fraud, abuse, laziness, a dependency culture and social irresponsibility encouraged by welfare dependency". If New Labour is to use and fund welfare – defined implicitly to mean social security benefits rather than 'the concept of the welfare state' – to attain the goal of social justice, then people have to believe that it works. Blair's pragmatic realism is evident:

> **... if people lose faith in welfare's ability to deliver, then politicians have an impossible job persuading hard-pressed taxpayers that their money should go on a system that is not working.**

Blair blames Conservative governments for helping to make welfare unpopular. They were committed to cutting welfare costs but "ended up increasing them". Moreover, as spending rose, so too did poverty and social exclusion. He suggests further that in cutting expenditure they sometimes created additional problems: "for example, encouraging fraud in their cuts to housing benefit". He might have added the hardship caused by cutting the relative, and occasionally the real, value of benefits (Walker).

Like Beveridge, Blair's aspiration is to make welfare a force for progress. His solution is "to reform it radically" by providing real security and opportunity, rooting out fraud and giving greatest help to those with the greatest needs.

The linking of targeting and rooting out fraud with providing real security is intriguing. It could be that, despite research-based evidence to the contrary (Walker), Blair believes that fraud and abuse are widespread[4]. Alternatively, he may be playing to popular mythology: public belief that abuse is rampant erodes confidence in the mutuality inherent in welfare and, hence, support for welfare (Toynbee). Lister recognises a danger in the latter strategy, warning "that the negative language used about benefits and benefit claimants could be counter-productive and divisive". To contrast a 'hand-up' with a 'hand-out', for example, makes good rhetoric but is hurtful to those who are on benefit through no fault of their own.

Similar dangers arise in the distinction that Blair draws between "real security" and "a welfare state that is just about 'social security'". Real security is to be achieved by accompanying benefits with active policies, justified on the grounds of enhancing opportunity. At the moment such policies are largely work-focused but Atkinson, Kellner, Lister and Walker all look to a time when these are extended to include other socially approved activities such as caring and community development. The danger is to presume, in the absence of good empirical evidence, that all traditional forms of social security 'encourage dependency'. To do so, as Blair recognises, causes "welfare – the good spending as well as the bad – to become stigmatised". In fact, as Blair also notes, Beveridge achieved much social good by providing people with their first retirement pension and peace of mind when unemployed. Security does not have to equate with dependency but active citizenship does depend on an adequate income. The goal of social security can often be achieved through the mechanism of social security. When it is, social security is likely to prove popular (Walker).

The modern vision

Blair's vision seeks to apply the core concepts of decency, merit, mutual responsibility and fairness and apply them to the modern world. It integrates an economic vision with a social one. The former builds a knowledge community on the foundation of stable economic management in which Britain competes on skill, talent and technology with "education being an economic and social imperative". It seems to reject the model in which British industry competes solely on price that is sometimes associated with approaches that seek primarily to enhance labour market flexibility. The social model has six characteristics:

- it tackles social exclusion, child poverty and community decay by tackling the fundamental causes;
- welfare is based on mutual responsibility with the state acting as an enabler and not just a provider;
- help goes to those most in need, using a mix of universal and targeted help;
- fraud and abuse are to be rooted out;

- public/private partnerships and the voluntary sector are to have an enhanced role in the delivery of welfare;
- active welfare provides services rather than just benefits.

Blair lists a number of policies that have already been implemented. These include those to get people back to work, to make work pay, to modernise public services, to tackle social decay, to provide security for those who have retired or cannot work, and to support children.

It would be unreasonable to expect a one-to-one correspondence between core concepts, characteristics and policies, but some observations are in order. First, though, it is worth noting that only one of the six characteristics is concerned with primary objectives, that is, with the reasons for establishing a welfare system – the giants to be slain. The others relate to secondary objectives, the means by which the failures of the pre-existing systems are to be overcome (for example, tackling fraud), and to the principles and mode of delivery. For Blair the twin subjects of social policy and social administration are as one; the policy and its delivery should be considered together as a whole.

Primary objectives

Overt and implicit support for the primary objectives and policies permeates the contributions to this volume. More is said below about the focus on childhood poverty. Tackling social exclusion by tackling its fundamental causes is as self-evidently sensible as it is difficult to achieve.

Contributors universally welcome the New Deal policies and the recognition that for many people paid work is "the best route out of poverty" (Lister) and "the main route through which individuals and families gain a sense of dignity, self-respect [and] a stake in society" (Plant). Likewise, policies that boost incomes in work – the minimum wage, the Working Families Tax Credit and other tax reforms that take low-income families out of tax – are singled out for praise. There is support, too, for polices that increase the incomes of the poorest pensioners and ensure that low wage earners are not condemned to poverty in old age. Similarly the creation of the Social Exclusion Unit at 'the heart of government' is lauded, as are policies to invest in low-income areas: New Deal for Communities, Employment, Education and Health Action Zones.

But, as would be expected, the contributors offer ideas that Blair has yet to adopt (of which more below). Moreover, they do not feel that government has always gone far enough. Nor do they necessarily agree with the particular strategies adopted or believe that they are risk-free. One concern with New Deal is that, as Piachaud quizzically notes, it "may obscure the fact that the government is firmly committed to security and a share in rising prosperity for those who cannot work". Firm commitment to those who cannot work is vital since significant numbers of welfare beneficiaries, even those of working age, are unlikely to be able to take the route from welfare to work (Walker). Moreover, Plant urges that Blair spells out the nature of the security to be offered to those who cannot work, and its foundation in relation to social justice and social inclusion. Giddens, for one, notes that "at any one time there are many people outside the labour market and government has an obligation to protect the vulnerable".

A second concern is that, as a result of substitution and displacement effects, as people on New Deal programmes find work more readily than those who do not and perhaps displace those already in employment, the net impact of Welfare to Work measures may be less than hoped for (Hills). Also, the improvement in incomes for some moving into work may not initially be great.

Yet another concern, one raised by Plant, is that, though correct, a work-orientated approach to social justice entails considerable and continuing expense. Yet despite this, Lister and Walker demand that such policies are extended to embrace the concept of sustainable employment, to break the 'low pay, no pay cycle' and to ensure that employment operates as a conveyor to ever-greater self-sufficiency.

Concerns raised about geographic targeting are twofold. First, and most importantly, such policies are simply inadequate when used in isolation since "most poor people live outside poor areas" (Piachaud). Second, the approach is insufficiently 'bottom-up', failing to allow for 'neighbourhood welfare' in which needy people run welfare for needy people (Holman). Lister generalises this latter point, arguing that the Social Exclusion Unit is not adequately participatory: the strategy should be to engage poor people and others who are excluded from the formal political debate in the development of policies to tackle social exclusion. She also argues that while the focus on discrete problems and groups may be necessary to ensure quick results, it risks:

> **... encouraging the belief that these groups are themselves 'the problem' and of obscuring the underlying processes and structures which lead to social exclusion....**

Similar structures and processes result in the spatial concentration of poverty and, to return to the first criticism of geographic targeting, these fundamental causes of social exclusion cannot solely be addressed by means of local policies.

The limited number of primary objectives listed by Blair is also noteworthy. The fact that there is no specific mention of poverty among groups other than children may simply reflect the emphasis given in the Lecture to announcing the intention to eradicate child poverty. Other groups are presumably subsumed under the category of socially excluded, though Deacon draws attention to the differentiated nature of poverty and warns of the necessity for differentiated responses.

The goals of fostering social cohesion and social solidarity are also notable by their absence. They would never be omitted from the list of policy objectives in continental Europe and lay at the heart of Beveridge's designs. Their omission may reveal a limited conception of popular welfare, one restricted to making the expenditure tolerable for the taxpayer rather than creating the belief of "everyone being in the same boat" in the way that Beveridge did (Harris). The danger is that mutuality is curtailed because of the emphasis in Blair's language on obligation rather than reciprocity, and that people are denied the same citizenship status when, at different stages in their lives, they are net recipients or givers. By downplaying the shared self-interest inherent in welfare, a chance is lost to capitalise on the "unique opportunity to create a constituency of support for building a more just society", and to make the positive case "for (fair) taxation as an expression of our responsibility to one another as citizens" (Lister).

Mechanisms

There is some disagreement between Blair and the contributors about the mechanisms by which help is to be targeted on those in most need. But before discussing this in more detail, attention should be drawn to the general support for other features of Blair's 'third way in welfare'.

As already noted, contributors largely share Blair's perspective on social justice, the priority to be given to equality of opportunity and the processes of social change. This, in turn, engenders support for the idea that welfare should not be limited to benefits, or even to benefits plus training. Instead, it should embrace active measures to improve health, education, housing and the infrastructure of community support for, as Plant remarks, "expecting people [with few skills] to become active in the labour market would be like compelling people to play football without being concerned whether they have football boots". Some contributors, notably but not only Kellner, argued to expand, or further define, welfare to include action to secure safe neighbourhoods, fair treatment by the police and courts, healthy and affordable food and access to information to hold authorities to account.

Likewise, the shared belief in the importance of mutual responsibility and/or mutuality, leads many contributors to consider, as Blair does, that individuals have a duty to make such provision as they are able for their own welfare and that of their families. Equally, the community has the duty to assist them. Contributors recognise, too, that the state is an important agent in the community's response but that it need not be the only player. Holman, as noted above, has great faith in the ability of neighbourhoods to respond, providing, that is, that they are adequately resourced. Beveridge, himself, believed strongly in the potential of state/voluntary sector self-governing partnerships, and although the great mutual organisations of the past are rapidly converting into private, commercial concerns, New Labour's welfare reforms look set to create a new generation of partnerships engaged in the delivery of welfare that involve public, voluntary and private enterprises.

Unlike Beveridge, neither Blair nor the contributors necessarily rule out a role for the commercial financial sector. Blair draws attention to Labour's strategy of building new public and private partnerships and to the role of the private sector in pensions provision and in New Deal programmes. Walker talks of social security as "community banking" and of "local franchises for service delivery". The state's role, in such circumstances, is that of enabler, strategic planner and regulator. Atkinson notes how, since Beveridge's time, the role of the state has changed from provider to regulator and that regulation in the economic field – rail pricing policy, for example – can be a major instrument in preventing social exclusion and fostering well-being. Again, emphasising the importance of regulation of the private sector, Kellner notes that the result of commercial logic and passive planning policy has been to create 'food deserts' in some inner urban areas due to the closure of small food outlets. As a consequence low-income families have less choice and higher food bills.

A number of contributors stress the reciprocal obligations that active policies impose on governments. Piachaud notes that to be successful "the Welfare to Work programme depends on full employment opportunities". Plant writes of the "moral imperative" to continue to fund such schemes and Walker argues that "obligations of welfare recipients should be accompanied by citizen rights to adequate benefits and a testable government commitment to quality service". The quid pro quo for enforcing individual obligations is enforceable accountability of government and/or its agents.

Some disparity of view emerges with respect to the issue of fraud and abuse: only Toynbee seems to attach a similar weight to that of Blair. Contributors would undoubtedly condemn those who engage in fraud and support Blair's intention to end "the systematic encouragement of fraud in the way the welfare state is designed". However, this is to return to the one area of significant contention between Blair and some of the contributors, the method of targeting on need. This is also Blair's major departure from the preferred strategy of Beveridge.

More important differences are apparent with regard to Blair's proposal of a mix of universal and targeted help and, particularly, his assertion that "the one is not 'superior' or 'more principled' than the other". The reforms introduced to date include increases in the level of universal benefits, notably Child Benefit, but also an extension of means testing in the benefit system and, with the series of new tax credits, via fiscal policy. Hills identifies, in the context of the means-tested Minimum Income Guarantee for pensions, the long-standing problem of low take-up[5]. Indeed, comprehensive take-up can probably only be achieved if benefits are paid automatically which, in turn, entails an element of compulsion (if only in the provision of information on income). But Lister and Deacon both believe that contributory benefits are generally superior to means testing. Lister argues that they better reflect "the spirit of a welfare contract and of the relationship between rights and responsibilities which informs the reform strategy", the view taken by Beveridge. In addition, Deacon draws attention to the interaction between contributory and means-tested benefits that can create the incentives that encourage people to abuse the system. One example is the way in which the Minimum Income Guarantee penalises savings. Another is provided by the plans to change Incapacity Benefit – a benefit paid in part to compensate for the extra costs of disability. The plan is to reduce benefits to recipients with occupational pensions, people "who have sought to act responsibly and make provision for themselves" (Deacon). As Piachaud acknowledges:

Focusing help on those in need through means-testing can reduce incentives to work and save. A balance must be found but the dilemma is inescapable.

Toynbee alone comes out explicitly against social insurance that she contends has always been "something of a con – a big idea, but muddled in reality. Its great advantage was to pretend to bind together the rich and the poor, to persuade the better-off to fund the system that paid out largely to the worse-off." The reason being "that then, as now, it would be too expensive and wasteful, to pay out non-means-tested entitlements at a rate that would cover a reasonable standard of living both to those who do, and those who don't, need it".

However, both Deacon and Lister acknowledge that Beveridge's original formulation of National Insurance is outdated since entitlement is based on contributions made by those in paid work. (Indeed, Beveridge himself recognised his own failure in this regard [Harris].) Equally, though, they believe a modern social insurance system is preferable "to a further move down the poverty relief model ... which has proved less successful than more comprehensive models in combating social exclusion and poverty". Alternatively, Atkinson suggests that Beveridge might favour a 'citizens income' or 'participation income' scheme, a universal cash payment paid to people on condition that they engage in socially recognised activities such as paid work, approved training or caring, or when they are absent from work for 'approved' reasons such as sickness or unemployment.

Ending child poverty

If the balance between means-tested and universal provision is a source of potential disagreement between Blair and the contributors, the commitment to end child poverty provides a basis for consensus. The reasons are many: common humanity and compassion; social justice and the emphasis on equality of opportunity; analysis and beliefs about the growth of childhood poverty and its individual and social consequences; and pragmatic concerns about cost and waste. Moreover, Atkinson reminds us that Beveridge took a similar view:

> **... the worst feature of Want in Britain is its concentration upon children [which] represents a destruction of human capital.**

The proportion of children in poverty has more than doubled in 20 years – the result of increases in lone parenthood, unemployment and worklessness – while recent research suggests its negative effects persist into adulthood in the form of poor qualifications, unemployment, low wages and increased contact with the police (Hills), poor physical and mental health and, even, teenage pregnancy (Piachaud, 1999). Moreover, social dynamics conspire to make children particularly vulnerable since, although long spells of poverty typically have more severe consequences than short ones, even transient periods of deprivation can be devastating for children when they coincide with key stages in biological development, education or peer group formation (Atkinson). If social justice is about equalising life chances, then childhood offers the first and most important chance that people get.

'Investing in children', Blair's term, is also used by Atkinson and Lister. Giddens, Hills, Le Grand and Piachaud identify the same priority. All see good education and healthcare as vital. They also single out for approval many of the policy tools that Blair cites: Child Benefit, Working Families Tax Credit, parental leave, childcare, Sure Start, the focus on school standards; and additional ones such as the higher Income Support for younger children and the acceptance of a maintenance disregard for those on Income Support that help the poorest children of all. Lister even suggests setting poverty reduction targets, though not explicitly with respect to children.

None, however, proposes the policy goal of eradicating child poverty, let alone set a date by which this should be achieved. It is interesting to ask 'why?' And 'why was Blair so bold?'

After a generation during which even the existence of poverty was denied, perhaps few truly believed that electoral considerations would allow any government to be anything but timid. While advocates of social democracy allow the state to intervene to foster social justice, they may have become conditioned to think 'intervene but not much'. Alternatively, aware both of the difficulties of definition and measurement, technical considerations perhaps blinded contributors to the possibilities. Yet again, maybe contributors felt that the policy tools that New Labour was prepared to use were inadequate. Or, perhaps they considered that no politician would be prepared to countenance the risk of failure.

Definitional issues are not mere academic niceties as Beveridge was very much aware (see also Chapter 16). He deliberately chose a poverty threshold only a little above Rowntree's 1899 primary poverty standard, albeit uprated for price inflation. Had he accepted Rowntree's higher 'Human Needs of Labour' poverty standard, designed to meet needs considered to be essential in the 1930s, he could not have claimed that his reforms would abolish want (Hills). Poverty thresholds need to change over time since rising public affluence makes life harder for those whose income is fixed in real terms. Therefore anti-poverty policy is necessarily directed at a moving target. Moreover, poverty measured in relative terms can only be eradicated by substantial income redistribution[6]. In their published responses to Blair's Lecture, Lister, Piachaud and Holman all question New Labour's willingness or ability to deliver such radical redistribution. Much of the positive redistribution that has taken place since 1997 has been achieved by stealth – presumably for fear of alienating public opinion. To be successful New Labour has actively to build a popular mandate for much more radical reform.

Labour may also have to develop new policy tools to complete the task. In Piachaud's estimation:

> **... improved education, expanded childcare, inspiring new programmes such as Sure Start for children at particular risk will all help. But to imagine that opportunities will be equalised in 20 years is scarcely realistic.**

He continues:

> **An end to child poverty requires an end to poverty in families. Better benefits for children can help, but ... ending child poverty [also] requires full employment. (Piachaud, 1999)**

On the other hand, as Holman (1999) also notes, Blair did not commit himself to either a concept or a measure of poverty, some yardstick against which the effectiveness of policy was to be assessed. Plant is clear that, as a Social Democrat, Blair should choose a relative rather than an absolute concept of poverty. However, he nevertheless presents this as a real choice for New Labour.

Politically, there must be great attraction in leaving the matter of definitions unaddressed. After all, much has already been achieved. A popular, socially including vision has been identified. A change of approach has been signalled, a modern response to a modern problem. Media reaction has been positive, if somewhat sceptical. Merely the call to end poverty could actively help to make welfare more popular. But, for the commitment to mutual responsibility to be sustained, public accountability is required which, in turn, demands a more precise statement of measurable objectives and a full consideration of the implications. The promised poverty audit will be an important test of Blair's political nerve and his commitment to mutual responsibility and social justice.

Omissions

Leaving aside the myriad of detailed observations and suggestions that find no place in Blair's lecture, three major issues warrant comment here. Perhaps Blair will address them on other occasions.

The first relates to the position of women, noted by Hills and Blair as one of the major determining changes in the last 50 years. There have been some important responses including the establishment of the Women's Unit and policies on the division of pension assets, childcare and parental leave entitlement. However, as Lister notes,

> **The changing position of women and the inappropriateness of a social security system still largely predicated on male unemployment patterns (in particular the assumption that people work either full time or not all) and a male breadwinner model ... and how caring responsibilities can best be recognised by the security system [are] only beginning to be addressed.**

Secondly, Blair failed to make any mention of the growing multi-cultural nature of British society. Poverty and many other forms of deprivation are disproportionately visited on particular minority ethnic groups. Therefore, to the extent that policies to eradicate poverty are successful, minority groups stand to make disproportionate gains. However, policies that are not differentiated to tackle the unique structural factors that cause certain minority groups to suffer higher levels of unemployment and deprivation will be of limited value and may even attenuate existing inequality. Neither the welfare system as a whole nor individual benefits are differentiated in this way. Moreover, evaluation of new benefit systems invariably fails to take explicit cognisance of the experience of minority ethnic groups, often simply because the samples used are too small to generate reliable estimates.

Thirdly, there is Europe. Achieving greater economic integration will inevitably generate social casualties, workers made unemployed through economic restructuring (Walker). The benefit system has to be robust enough to protect people and adequately to prepare and support them in new forms of employment. Equally, Europe is an opportunity to promote the integration of social and economic policy. It also affords the possibility of establishing social targets to be addressed collectively. Atkinson suggests a minimum level of Child Benefit mandated on member states, while Lister notes that the United Nations Copenhagen Summit agreed an explicit poverty reduction target.

Dimensions of the debate

Blair offers a vision of welfare for the 21st century and the explicit policy goal to end child poverty. The vision is built on a concept of social justice that has equality of opportunity at its core and mutual responsibility as a motor. The state is active in the promotion of social justice, an enabler and a provider in a mixed economy of welfare that seeks to focus help on those most in need. The system is modern in that it is well adapted to current economic imperatives and prevailing social mores. It is popular in that sufficient funds can be released through the democratic process to meet set priorities. The objective to end child poverty is just. It also seems that it is popular.

Blair believes that Beveridge would share his vision. He might. Both share a belief in prudent financing, integrated social and economic policies, the relief of poverty, compulsory minimum benefits, personal saving, obligations in return for benefits, provision of services as well as benefits and child allowances to improve work incentives and relieve child poverty (Harris). However, Beveridge believed full employment to be an essential prerequisite of social justice, something that Blair believes is an unattainable goal in a global economy. Beveridge also considered social insurance to be preferable to selectivity, whereas in principle Blair is agnostic though more of a selectivist in practice.

Beveridge, of course, offered a blueprint; Blair has so far played the role of visionary. Some new policies have been put in place. Most are consistent with the new vision. But further policy prescriptions are likely to be needed if childhood poverty is to be eradicated. If not a blueprint, then a large-scale map is definitely required. Such a map would need to add other policy goals to the eradication of child poverty that were consistent with equal opportunity and social justice. Should we not end poverty in old age, among disabled people, among whichever groups are affected and wherever it occurs? Should we not tackle all social barriers to opportunity? If not, should we not be explicit about the priorities and criteria for establishing them? Such are some of the dimensions of the debate.

There are other, even more fundamental, ones. Blair and Beveridge may be radical reformers but both are evolutionary rather than revolutionaries. Their approach is to develop and refine existing structures. They have accepted the premise that the principal aim of welfare is the relief and prevention of poverty. The goals of social solidarity and social cohesion are much less important, and less important than they are in much of continental Europe. Both accept an important role for the state, but implementation is inherently and increasingly individualistic: policies encourage people to save for themselves rather than for each other. Policy design and implementation is also top-down. Lister, Holman and Kellner offer various other models in which needy and other citizens participate in the design, auditing and/or delivery of welfare. Are these alternatives preferable? Do they challenge the prevailing social democratic conception of justice? Would they result in different objectives and alternative priorities? Are they more or less attuned with the dynamic, uncertain, variegated and individualistic society that defines the beginning of the 21st century? Would they excite media interest and challenge popularist beliefs about the nature and causes of poverty and the most appropriate policy solutions (Chapter 16)?

Blair's radicalism has begun to challenge the once prevailing view that government is impotent in the face of market forces, that social justice is an unattainable ideal. His vision is of a proactive role for policy, changing individual behaviour and social structures to facilitate justice and progress. In shaping this vision, Blair drew heavily on the ideas and aspirations of others. It must be assumed that he will continue to do so as the vision is refined and the policies are developed. Readers of this volume are invited to engage with Blair's ideas and to contribute to the ongoing debate. Welfare is important for every citizen and for democracy itself.

Notes

[1] Income Support for pensioners is to be uprated in line with wages as part of the Minimum Income Guarantee.

[2] It is interesting to speculate whether Blair would take a different view in light of the opposition of Labour backbenchers to proposals to reform disability benefits during consideration of the Welfare Reform Bill in May 1999.

[3] A letter purporting to represent the views of 150 delegates at the Social Policy Association conference was published in *The Guardian* on 31 July 1998, a response to consultation on the Green Paper *A new contract for welfare*. It welcomed "the practice of consultation and the broad canvas of the Paper's concerns" but noted that the "Americanised use of the term 'welfare'" was "both confusing and damagingly divisive". It reported "considerable concern"

about "the way the principle of 'work for those who can, security for those who cannot' had been translated into specific proposals". It was also critical of "what the Green Paper had to offer" on the adequacy of benefit levels and the absence of suggestions for updating the male breadwinner model of social security. It concluded that there was an "absence of a clear and comprehensive strategy for the reform of the overall structure of social security". The letter is reproduced in *SPA News*, October/November 1998, pp 2-3.

[4] Official measures of fraud are suspect since they do not require uncontrovertible evidence. Moreover, while such studies show substantial sums lost through fraud, they also indicate that the vast majority of benefit recipients are not fraudulent.

[5] Errors have recently been discovered in official estimates of take-up which mean that the extent of take-up among pensioners has been overstated. Even so, the new estimates suggest that between 400,000 and 700,000 pensioners were not claiming the Income Support due to them in 1996/97.

[6] This is so for the following reasons. First, as already noted, the poverty threshold is a moving target that drifts upwards following average incomes. Second, social and political sensibilities mean that the poverty threshold will probably always be pitched above the income level that low-skilled people can attain through paid employment (or life-time savings). The degree of inequality implied by setting it any lower is likely to be politically unacceptable (probably because it is also considered to be socially dangerous). It follows that economic growth and rising real wages provide no solution to the existence of poverty. The only other strategy is to redistribute income from persons above the poverty threshold to those beneath it. This can be achieved in various ways including adjustments to the minimum wage, more progressive taxation and higher benefit levels to name three direct methods.

References

DSS (Department of Social Security) (1999) *Income related benefits estimates of take-up*, London: DSS; Analytic Services Division 3; available at www.dss.gov.uk/hq.

Holman, B. (1999) 'Limited imagination', *The Guardian*, Society, 31 March.

Piachaud, D. (1999) 'Means to an end', *The Guardian*, Society, 31 March.

Further reading

Atkinson, A.B. (1995) *Incomes and the welfare state*, Cambridge: Cambridge University Press.

Atkinson, A.B. (1998) *Poverty in Europe*, Oxford: Basil Blackwell.

Atkinson, A.B. (1999) *The economic consequences of rolling back the welfare state*, Cambridge, MA: MIT Press.

Bennett, F. and Walker, R. (1998) *Working with work*, York: York Publishing Services for the Joseph Rowntree Foundation.

Deacon, A. (1997) 'Benefit sanctions for the jobless: "tough love" or rough treatment? Employment Policy Institute Economic Report, vol 11, no 7, pp 1-8.

Deacon, A. (1998) 'The Green Paper on welfare reform: a case for enlightened self-interest?' *Political Quarterly*, vol 69, no 3, pp 306-11.

Deacon, A. (1999: forthcoming) 'Dependency and inequality: a false polarity in the poverty debate?' *Journal of Social Policy*, vol 27, no 4.

Deacon, A. (2000: forthcoming) 'Learning from the USA? The influence of American ideas upon "New Labour" thinking on welfare reform', *Policy & Politics*, forthcoming. Originally delivered as the paper 'Welfare reform in the 51st state: American influences upon the welfare debate in Britain' at the 20th Research Conference of the Association for Public Policy Analysis and Management, New York City, October 1998.

Deacon, A. and Mann, K. (1999) 'Moralism and modernity: The paradox of New Labour thinking on welfare' *Benefits*, no 20, pp 2-6.

Giddens, A. (1998) *The third way*, Cambridge: Polity Press.

Harris, J. (1997) *William Beveridge: A biography, 2nd edition*, Oxford, New York: Clarendon Press (paperback, 1997).

Hills, J. (1995) *Inquiry into income and wealth, volume 2: A summary of the evidence*, York: Joseph Rowntree Foundation.

Hills, J. (ed) (1996) *New inequalities: The changing distribution of income and wealth in the UK*, Cambridge: Cambridge University Press.

Hills, J. (1998) *Income and wealth: The latest evidence*, York: Joseph Rowntree Foundation.

Hills, J., Ditch, J. and Glennerster, H. (eds) (1994) *Beveridge and social security: An international retrospective*, Oxford: Oxford University Press.

Holman, B. (1997) *Towards equality: A Christian manifesto*, Reading: SPCK.

Holman, B. (1997) *FARE dealing: Neighbourhood involvement in a housing scheme*, London: Community Development Foundation.

Holman, B. (ed) (1998) *Faith in the poor*, Oxford: Lion Publishing.

Holman, B., Timms, S. and Stanton, H. (1999) *Joined up writing: New Labour and social exclusion*, London: Christian Socialist Movement Pamphlet.

Le Grand, J. (1984) 'Equity as an economic objective', *Journal of Applied Philosophy*, vol 1, pp 39-51. Reprinted in B. Almond and D. Hill (eds) *Applied philosophy: Morals and metaphysics in contemporary debate*, London: Routledge 1991.

Le Grand, J. (1989) 'Markets, equality and welfare,' in J. Le Grand and S. Estrin (eds) *Market socialism*, Oxford: Oxford University Press, pp 193-211.

Le Grand, J. (1991) *Equity and choice*, London: Harper Collins (especially Chapters 4, 5 and 6).

Lister, R. (1997) 'From fractured Britain to one nation?: The policy options for welfare reform', *Renewal*, vol 5, nos 3 and 4, pp 11-23.

Lister, R. (1998) 'Making welfare work', in W. Stevenson (ed) *Equality and the modern economy, No 2*, London: The Smith Institute, pp 15-22.

Lister, R. (1998) 'New conceptions of citizenship,' in N. Ellison and C. Pierson (eds) *Developments in British social policy*, Basingstoke: Macmillan, pp 46-60.

Lister, R. (1999) 'What welfare provisions do women need in order to become full citizens?', in S. Walby (ed) *New agendas for women*, Basingstoke: Macmillan, pp 17-31.

Lister, R. (forthcoming) 'Strategies for social inclusion: promoting social cohesion or social justice?', in P. Askonas and A. Stewart (eds) *Social Inclusion: Possibilities and tension*, Basingstoke: Macmillan.

Piachaud, D. (1996) *The price of food: Missing out on mass consumption*, London; STICERD, Occasional Paper, 20, London School of Economics.

Piachaud, D. (1997) 'A price worth paying? The costs of unemployment', in J. Philpott (ed) *Working for full employment*, London: Routledge, pp 49-62.

Piachaud, D. (1997) 'The growth of means-testing', in A. Walker and C. Walker (eds) *Britain divided*, London: Child Poverty Action Group, pp 75-83.

Piachaud, D. (1997) 'Social security and dependence,' *International Social Security Review*, vol 50, no 1, pp 41-55.

Piachaud, D. (1998) 'Prospects for poverty,' *New Economy*, vol 5, no 1, pp 8-13.

Plant, R. (1991) *Modern political thought*, Oxford: Blackwell.

Plant, R. (1993) 'Hayek on social injustice: a critique', in J. Birner and R. von Zijp (eds) *Hayek: Co-ordination and evolution: His legacy in philosophy, politics, economics and the history of ideas*, London, New York: Routledge.

Plant, R. (1998) *New Labour: A third way?*, London: European Policy Forum.

Plant, R., Lesser, H. and Taylor Gooby, P. (1980) *Political philosophy and social welfare: Essays on the normative basis of welfare provision*, London: Routledge and Kegan Paul.

Leisering, L. and Walker, R. (eds), (1998) *The dynamics of modern society: Poverty, policy and welfare*, Bristol: The Policy Press.

Vincent, A. and Plant, R. (1984) *Philosophy politics and citizenship: The life and thought of British idealists*, Oxford: Blackwell.

Walker, R. (1998) 'The Americanisation of British welfare: a case study of policy transfer', *Focus*, Journal of the Institute for Research on Poverty, University of Madison-Wisconsin, vol 19, no 3, pp 32-40; to be reprinted in the *International Journal of Health Services*.

Walker, R. (1998) 'Promoting positive welfare', *New Economics*, vol 5, no 2, pp 77-82.

Walker, R. and Park, J. (1998) 'Unpicking poverty', in C. Oppenheim (ed) *An inclusive society*, London: IPPR, pp 29-52.

Index

Note: contributors, quotations and some passing references have not been included in this index.

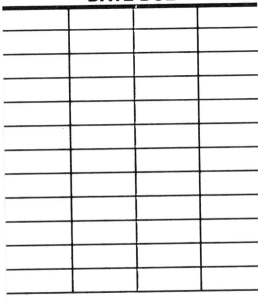